A Moon for the Misbegotten

# A Moon for the Misbegotten

## Eugene O'Neill

*With an Introduction by*
Stephen A. Black

YALE NOTA BENE

*Yale University Press   New Haven and London*

First published as a Yale Nota Bene book in 2006.

For information about this and other Yale University Press publications, please
contact:

| U.S. office | sales.press@yale.edu |
| Europe office | sales@yaleup.co.uk |

Set in Garamond type by Tseng Information Systems, Inc.
Printed in the United States of America.

Library of Congress Control Number: 2006903366
ISBN-13: 978-0-300-11815-5
ISBN-10: 0-300-11815-5

A catalogue record for this book is available from the British Library.

10  9  8  7  6  5  4  3  2  1

# Introduction
## Eugene O'Neill and *A Moon for the Misbegotten*
### STEPHEN A. BLACK

Of O'Neill's major plays, the two most often performed and most often read by the general public and in English or drama courses are probably *Long Day's Journey into Night* and its sequel, *A Moon for the Misbegotten*. *Long Day's Journey* was immediately recognized as a great work at its 1956 debut. *Moon* took much longer to have its great value acknowledged and to find its place among O'Neill's plays and in the canon of American drama. The Theatre Guild attempted a production in 1947, which closed after trial performances in Columbus, St. Louis, and Detroit (where censors wanted to close the play for blasphemy), and it was not performed in the United States again until 1957 (although a fairly successful production played in Belfast and Dublin in 1954).

It is not surprising that *Long Day's Journey* was so quickly accepted, because of the well-publicized knowledge that O'Neill had tried to ensure that the play would never be performed, and never be published in his lifetime. O'Neill's efforts implied that the intimate details of family life with a mother addicted to morphine were scandalously true, and that the story revealed much about the personal life of a playwright who had done his best throughout his life to guard his privacy. That *Journey* was a great play was also immediately visible. It was as inescapably powerful and disturbing in its effect as that other great family play, *King Lear,* and as unforgettable.

*Moon* is a different and much more difficult play to grasp. It begins as a broad comedy of rough country manners, and then transforms into the somber story of a man compulsively telling a young woman, a reluctant listener, of his behavior—behavior he can neither forget nor forgive himself—while his mother was dying in Los Angeles, and while he accompanied her body on the train to New York. The man is called Jim Tyrone and is the same character as the older brother in *Long Day's Journey*. The story is set eleven years after the time of *Journey*, a few weeks before the actual James O'Neill, Jr., the playwright's older brother, died in a private asylum from prolonged alcohol poisoning. *Moon* is a kind of sequel to *Long Day's Journey*, but the connection would not be apparent for another nine years because even the existence, let alone the story, of *Journey* would not be known until 1956, long after *Moon* had its unsuccessful 1947 tryout. The years immediately after World War II were not propitious for long, somber, tragic plays.

By 1956 the world had changed. *Journey* won immediate recognition. Its New York opening, directed by José Quintero, with Frederick March, Florence Eldridge, Jason Robards, Bradford Dillman, and Kathleen Ross, worked wonderfully, holding audiences spellbound for its full four-hour length and sending them from theaters with that mixture of somberness and elation that lets us know we have had an experience that has in some way changed our lives.

*Moon* has had a quite different history. The play's progression from amusing to disturbing led at first to some confused productions and audiences. After several productions in America and the British Isles, the play finally began to come into its own and to seem coherent because of a production in 1973, directed by Quintero and starring Jason Robards as Jim Tyrone. Robards, who had played the older brother, Jamie, in *Journey*, was now playing a Jamie eleven years older. Unable to mourn and begin the letting go that must happen after a death, unable to stop thinking about his dead father and mother, cut off from his brother, Jamie was much further gone in alcoholism and despair than ever before. In Colleen Dewhurst, the role of Josie had a gifted actress who was approximately the size and appearance O'Neill specified for the other main character. Ed Flanders played Phil Hogan. The production, filmed for television with the same actors and broadcast by ABC in 1975, is available to educational institutions and has become widely known. It seems likely that O'Neill would have been satisfied with the production—to the degree he was ever satisfied with any of his plays on stage—and many O'Neill scholars and enthusiasts think of it as the definitive production. It has surely been a source of emulation as well as imitation for directors and actors who put on the play. That may be a mixed blessing for many reasons, only one of which is that no one else can be Mr. Robards or Ms. Dewhurst. It is possible that the influence of the Quintero-Robards-Dewhurst production has inhibited directors and actors from exploring some of the play's possibilities.

An O'Neill scholar and man of the theater, Paul Voelker, who had seen Robards and Dewhurst only in the television version, wrote in 1978, with perhaps a little exaggeration, that simply because Robards is Robards, Jim Tyrone becomes the most important character in the play, when he should not be "even the second most important." Voelker felt that simply casting Robards as Tyrone gave the part such weight, emphasizing so very strongly Jim's self-loathing as he described his misbehavior with the prostitute on the train, that it overbalanced the play and reduced it to little more than an autobiographical document. Voelker is surely correct when he writes that Jim's confessional speech is no more important than Josie's reaction to it, although I think there is much more to say on the point.

I believe that understanding Jim enables Josie finally to acknowledge a desire for love from a man she can admire, a desire that she has denied herself because she takes for granted that she is unattractive and because she gets a good deal of satisfaction from her life of working the farm, being housekeeper and almost a wife to her father, and being co-prankster in his schemes and practical jokes. When she is forced to listen to Jim in acts 3 and 4, he makes her understand what she doesn't want to know: that Jim really means it, and really understands what he says, when he repeatedly tells her that he is "dead." Josie has insisted (as the audience is likely to do at first) on interpreting the words to mean, perhaps, that he feels like hell or has a terrible hangover. She must now understand that Jim is emotionally dead, even if he will continue to breathe for a little while longer, that he is incapable of giving her the kind of love that she has finally admitted to herself she needs and wants—the kind she can't get from a father, no matter how much he loves her and no matter how much fun they get from their jokes and games.

And so one can say that the play ends with a loss, the loss by Josie of her comforting back-of-the-mind assumption that she loves Jim Tyrone and he might be made to love her sometime if things get rocky enough for him that he needs a soft, womanly bosom to weep on. Her father has held a slightly different notion for some time, that if he can catch Jim at just the right moment, a moment like tonight, say, when he's blue and the heebie-jeebies are after him, that perhaps Jim might see how fine Josie's qualities are, that she might even make him happy for a while, or as happy as he can be, and that he might even wander into marrying her.

But that loss is much less for Josie than another, even deeper loss. She loses the pseudo-self she has created to protect her from feeling sorry for herself, for thinking herself "a great cow of a woman," as she says. Without that, she has to confront a world of choices and possibilities that she seems largely to have ignored, the most important of which is that her life and future will require many more decisions than she has considered, much less chosen or agreed to.

Forced to confront her pipe dream version of Jim, Josie cannot avoid looking at the needs within her that made her have the pipe dreams and that kept her contented with her life on the farm with Phil. It's not a bad life, all in all. But she's had a glimpse of something else: not life with some farmhand or some town man, not even life with a man like Jim, but a life with possibilities she can't anticipate or predict. The most prominent thing she has to confront is nothing less than death itself. As she gradually realizes that Jim is truly approaching physical death, she has to accept the reality of death in general: her father will die, she will die, everything will change, suddenly or gradually. It is the beginning of considering herself and growing into herself.

This is some of what she must think and imagine as she spends the long, cramped night holding her dead child, Jim, in her arms, and waking—miracle of miracles—still a virgin. Accepting that Jim cannot love her or anyone and that he wants only to die seems to crystallize whatever process of growth has been going on in Josie during the years of watching her father evict his sons from the family farm, and to free her from whatever has made her cling to being her father's daughter. At twenty-eight she finally grows into her real age and is perhaps ready to let herself be a grown woman. Josie's growth into knowing and accepting herself is the story of the play as much as or more than Jim's confession and his approaching, self-willed death.

In June 1939, O'Neill had been suffering increasingly poor health for about five years. After living in Sea Island, Georgia, for nearly two years, he found he could not tolerate the heat or humidity, which seemed to exacerbate various health problems. A series of inconclusive medical consultations in New York convinced him to seek a milder climate, and so the O'Neills moved to the West Coast in 1936. In November they arrived in Seattle, where O'Neill had a good friend, Sophus Winther, an English professor at the University of Washington who had written a book about his plays that he liked. Shortly after they arrived it was announced that O'Neill had won the Nobel Prize for Literature.

In December they moved to the San Francisco Bay area, where Carlotta had spent her childhood and where her mother, daughter, and son-in-law lived. Within days of their arrival, while staying at the Fairmont in San Francisco, O'Neill developed acute abdominal pain, was diagnosed with acute appendicitis, and was moved to Merritt Hospital in Oakland, where he underwent emergency surgery. Complications developed, and he nearly died. He remained in the hospital until March 1, 1937, and the Nobel Prize was brought to the hospital and presented by the Swedish Consul to San Francisco, with Carlotta and several nurses for witnesses. From this point on, O'Neill would never have a day without having to think about various chronic medical problems.

Among the several ailments was a tremor which was misdiagnosed as Parkinson's disease, or "atypical Parkinson's disease." In Parkinson's, the tremor is worse when one is at rest and reduces as a person tries to do something; in O'Neill, the tremor became worse as he tried to do something, such as form letters with a pencil. The issue was confused because O'Neill had since childhood had a so-called "intention" or "familial" tremor, assumed to be inherited from his mother, who also had it. Apparently, the family tremor was unrelated to the increasingly severe tremor that developed in O'Neill's forties. An autopsy eventually showed that Purkinje's cells, large cells in the middle layer of the cerebral cortex that control fine movements, were rapidly dying off because of some unknown degenerative process, so that when he died he had only a small fraction of the number of the cells that would have been expected in the brain of a man of sixty-five, his age at death.

The esoteric medical situation had an immediate, practical effect on O'Neill's life: it threatened his ability to continue writing. The extinction of the cells, which control fine motor coordination, affected O'Neill's ability to perform many ordinary actions, such as lifting food to his mouth, swallowing, walking, and especially writing by hand. Like many writers, O'Neill was able to compose in only one way. Although he could type, he could not compose at the typewriter, and neither could he learn to compose by dictating to a secretary or a machine. In the late 1930s O'Neill had to accept that, even though he continued to get ideas for new plays with his usual remarkable fecundity, his days of actually being able to write what he conceived were numbered.

In addition to his health problems, the world situation greatly affected both him and Carlotta. Hitler had overrun Czechoslovakia and Poland and was preparing to invade France, where the O'Neills had lived from 1928 to 1931. In 1939 America was still recovering from the Great Depression and few Americans believed the country should become involved in the war developing in Europe or even showed much interest in it, a condition that changed little until Pearl Harbor was attacked. Because the O'Neills had lived in France, war was much more real to them. The phrase "war obsession" occurred almost daily in O'Neill's diaries, and Carlotta also frequently mentioned the war in her diaries. She describes them listening to the bad news on a shortwave radio that they had on almost constantly, listening through the static and fading signals for something that sounded like a fact. At this time, using money from the sale of their house in Georgia and from the Nobel Prize, the O'Neills built a Spanish-style house on a fine 158-acre property in the hills on the east side of San Francisco Bay, near the town of Danville. Here they would live until the late days of World War II, when shortages of gasoline and other essentials made continued living in isolation impractical for two aging people with serious health problems.

With the world and his health unsettled, O'Neill felt a particular urgency to complete certain projects while he was able, ideas he had long considered for plays but had never felt ready to write. These were the plays now known as the "late plays."

On June 6, 1939, he wrote in his *Work Diary:* "decide do outlines of [*The Iceman Cometh*] idea and N[ew]. L[ondon]. family one"— that is, *Long Day's Journey.* He wrote both outlines in the next few weeks and then wrote *Iceman* first, completing two drafts by the following January. He then reread the outline for *Journey* that he had written almost a year before. He put off beginning it, knowing the emotional toll that writing it would take from him. In June 1940, he returned to *Journey* and found his draft of act 1 better than he had expected. "Deeply moved," he noted, "convinced I can make it one of my best." From then on he wrote every day and finished it on his 52nd birthday, October 16, 1940, three weeks before Pearl Harbor. In April 1941, he began the wonderful one-act play *Hughie,* which he drafted in about three weeks. On May 16, after a bit of revising, he called it finished and wrote, "had a lot of fun doing this and like it." Next he rewrote a play first drafted while they lived in Georgia, *A Touch of the Poet,* and also sketched several other play ideas, some in considerable detail, that he never finished.

On October 28 he wrote in his diary, "(S[haughnessy] play idea based on story E[dmond] tells in 1st act of 'L.D.J.I.N' except here Jamie principal character & story of play otherwise entirely imaginary except for Jamie's revelation of self)." (Shaughnessy is the name given in *Journey* for the character who became Phil Hogan.) The next day he wrote of the idea, "this can be strange combination comic-tragic—am enthused about it." He made a sketchy outline of acts 1 and 2 the next day, then began detailed outlines of acts 3 and 4, which he finished on November 3, despite acute pain from prostatitis, one of his many ailments.

In November and early December he wrote short drafts of acts 1 and 2, and he had just begun act 3 when, on Sunday, December 7, much of America's Pacific fleet was damaged or destroyed in the bombing of Pearl Harbor. O'Neill wrote, "[N]ow the whole world goes into the tunnel!—but this has to be—we should have beaten the bastards to the punch! [G]lued to radio." On the 10th, he returned to act 3: "am determined to finish 1st draft of this play, war or not. The Archimedes viewpoint should be the artist's, (as long as he is physically out, anyway—stick to one's job)." By January 20, 1942, he had finished much more detailed drafts of acts 3 and 4 than the drafts of acts 1 and 2, then put the play aside. He worked off and on at several ideas never developed, then began revising *A Touch of the Poet* at the end of October 1942. In December he returned to *Moon* and worked steadily on the second draft of act 4, continuing through May 3, 1943, when the surviving diary breaks off.

O'Neill liked the play very much. After the war had ended and *The Iceman Cometh,* playing to mixed reviews, ran for 136 performances in the winter of 1946–47, he wanted to have *Moon* performed, and he cooperated as fully as his failing health allowed with the Theatre Guild's plans for a production. He was particularly interested in the casting of Josie, whom he portrays in an act 1 character description as being "almost a freak—five feet eleven in her stockings . . . with large, firm breasts . . . [and] long smooth arms, immensely strong, although no muscles show . . . [and] no mannish quality." After interviewing many actresses, he chose Mary Welch, an actress of ordinary size, simply because she convinced him she understood the part and the play, and because she was Irish.

A tryout run in Columbus, St. Louis, and Detroit was not encouraging, and Theatre Guild dropped the project. The play was not performed again in America for ten years, and that did not succeed either, despite a very strong review in the *New York Post* by Richard Watts, who particularly praised the performances by Wendy Hiller and Franchot Tone. It ran for only 68 performances. A revival at the Circle in the Square in 1968, with Salome Jens and Mitchell Ryan, ran 199 performances, but did not lead to other productions. Five years later, in 1973, the José Quintero production finally began to establish *Moon* in the public mind as one of O'Neill's important plays. But as Paul Voelker's comments suggest, it seems fair to say that the play was still not well understood.

The thesis of my biography of O'Neill (*Eugene O'Neill, Beyond Mourning and Tragedy,* 1999) is that for various reasons it took a very long time for O'Neill to pass through the process of mourning after the deaths, in a little more than three years, of all the other members of his parental family. His father died a slow and painful death from abdominal cancer in August 1920; about eighteen months later, his mother, apparently in good health and free for six years of her morphine addiction, died suddenly of a brain tumor; and a little more than eight months after his mother died, his brother succeeded in doing what he had told everyone he meant to do: he died in an alcohol-induced coma in an asylum.

The process of grieving is described by different authorities as a series of stages, beginning with denial of the loss, followed by a long process of gradually accepting the reality of a world that no longer includes those on whom, in one way or another, one has depended, and ending, for some, with a letting go that is possible because one has grown by surviving the ordeal into a new degree of independence and capability.

For O'Neill the process of mourning took an extraordinarily long time, partly because the deaths came so close together, and more because O'Neill was past thirty before he began to reach a state of independence from his parents and brother. To a considerable extent, the act of writing *Long Day's Journey* enabled O'Neill to consolidate the process of mourning that had, in the 1920s, led him into at least three attempts at psychoanalysis. O'Neill continued the process begun with the analysts by writing his plays of the 1920s, most of them directly or indirectly informed by psychoanalysis: *Welded, All God's Chillun Got Wings, Desire Under the Elms, The Great God Brown, Strange Interlude, Lazarus Laughed, Dynamo, Mourning Becomes Electra,* and *Days Without End.* Almost all of them represent either the lost members of his family or other aspects of mourning. This process culminated, beginning in the late 1930s, in the writing of plays directly based on people and events from his youth, beginning with *The Iceman Cometh.* In *Long Day's Journey* O'Neill represented as truthfully as he could the way life seemed to him, in retrospect, in his parental home, using not only memories of the past but the present understanding of a fifty-two-year-old man (one who, by the way, was dealing, not very well, with the problems of his own three children). In writing *Journey,* O'Neill seems to have made some progress in understanding and accepting his mother and especially his father. His brother posed much greater problems for him.

Everything we know historically about O'Neill, and everything we find in *Journey* and in the many autobiographical elements in his other plays suggests that to Eugene, while growing up, Jamie seemed the one reasonable person, the one with common sense, in a family where reason and common sense were rare. Even harder than accepting his mother's morphine addiction, even harder than accepting his father's miserliness and other quirks, was accepting what he had to see in his brother after his mother had died.

And so he created an outsider, Josie Hogan, who grew in a single night to discover what an insider took twenty years to learn — twenty years because he had needed so much to believe that one person in his family saw clearly and told the truth about the family craziness. Nothing was harder for O'Neill than learning that beneath his brother's apparent good humor and common sense was a dreadful emptiness. That emptiness, that nothingness, that Black Hole of Calcutta inside, is what he had to know and understand to create the character of Jamie in *Long Day's Journey,* and that is what he finally got fully into focus in creating Jim Tyrone in *Moon.* He had to do it, not to justify himself, not even just to understand Jim, but to be able to accept that Jim was the man he was. O'Neill had to do this in order to relinquish an inner image that was part of himself, a self-destructive part of himself. That is what it meant to O'Neill that he could finally write *A Moon for the Misbegotten.*

I hope, but am not entirely sure, that understanding something about the creative process that led to the existence of *Moon* will always be helpful not only to readers but also to actors and directors putting on the play. I suspect that being able to go, by an act of empathy, to that potential place of darkness or emptiness within one's self — and survive to return from the trip! — is a prerequisite for directing the play or for playing Jim or Josie in a deeply meaningful way. It is something I have seen a few times in performances of *Moon,* and not only by Jason Robards.

Almost as much is required of an actor playing Josie as of one playing Jim. In the long run, I think whether she is almost six feet tall and looks as strong as most men matters not nearly so much as whether she can let herself have at least a notion of what Jim's inner darkness looks and feels like. Above all she must convince us that she grows visibly as the reality of Jim's dreadful story has its cumulative effect on her and on the audience. She must convince us that she understands that Jim is not just some conscienceless monster who cannot feel what others consider to be a normal feeling: the guilt he experiences when he obsessively repeats his story of his behavior during and after his mother's dying. Jim's particular burden is to know well what it means to be fully human, and to find himself, time after time, inadequate when anyone else demands from him what he needs from others. That is what Josie understands by the end of her long journey into the night as she holds the dying Jim in her arms and when she finds him still alive at dawn, and herself still a virgin. That is the joke of the moon.

We have known since the time of Aristotle that when we attempt to describe the tragic, the best we can hope to do is to draw analogies that might be useful in describing what is ultimately a subjective matter, the effect of witnessing a particular work. It is somehow illuminating, for example, to consider the many resemblances between the situation of Aeschylus's Orestes and that of Hamlet; perhaps such an analogy subjectively leads us to grasp more of the qualities of each work by thinking of their similarities. The classicist M. Owen Lee has written an attractive monograph, *Athena Sings* (2003), which draws analogies between the *Oresteia* of Aeschylus and Wagner's *Ring,* and persuades me that Wagner had Aeschylus in mind when he created his versions of the Nordic gods and their world.

In *The Tragic Plane* (1985), H. A. Mason explicitly abandons "normal modes of definition" and substitutes paradoxes and impressions for more conventional approaches to describing that elusive thing, tragedy. He asks us to hypothesize being taken to a plane different from that which we occupy daily, one where we can consider as co-existing such contradictory propositions as "Tragedy must be religious" and "Tragedy cannot be religious," or "Tragedy is an affair of men" and "Tragedy is the concern of the gods" (p. v). In part Mason believes that although we cannot define it, we know dramatic tragedy when we experience it; we know we are on that plane of experience. On the tragic plane, Mason says, "We are required to confront terrors and desires" beyond which we believe humanity has progressed in our social and economic evolution, terrors and desires we believe no longer beset us as they did our primal ancestors.

Historians of ancient Greek civilization and art point out that Greek tragedies, like the Greek myths and Homeric episodes they are usually based on, look back to the gods and a way of seeing the world that conflicted with the great developments in natural sciences, mathematics, rhetoric, history, and philosophy, as well as in the arts, which have led to that era being called "Classical" and to the phrase "Classical Humanism." By the last half of the fifth century B.C.E., the Olympian gods were beginning to be objects of mockery (as recorded in the satires of Aristophanes and some of the "satyr" plays that survive as larger fragments). At the same time, belief continued in the Olympian gods, and their shrines continued to be active, coexisting with scientific explanations of life and nature, of cause and effect, and with Plato's Academy.

The questions in the tragedies of why things happen appear to reveal at crucial times that cause and effect are of the gods and inaccessible to human thought or senses. The younger Oedipus had to believe that the power to evade his prophesied fate rested in his own mind and decisions. Not to believe that would make him feel helpless to a degree that we can barely imagine, let alone tolerate knowing. But in the past 150 years or so we have been forced repeatedly to tolerate discoveries by the priests of our modern gods that we have relatively little ability to know—let alone to control—the future or even our present circumstances: such control is basic to what we, like the ancient Greeks, think of as "humanism."

The conflict between the religious and the humanistic is made especially clear in two of the last written of the great classical tragedies, *Bakkhai,* written by Euripides in about 407, near the end of his long life, and *Oedipus at Colonos,* written in 406 by an even older Sophocles. Both plays are as anachronistic as they can possibly be in harking back to ways of thinking about the forces of life that had been widely accepted for decades as outmoded. Each of the plays, in its way, constitutes a profoundly religious argument against the rationalism that had come to dominate Greek civilization. Plato's famous distrust of the poets rested on his commitment to the rationalism fundamental to Western philosophy, of which he was the leading pioneer. The distrust was mutual. The tragic poets held an equally deep distrust of the purely humanistic, distrust that is everywhere evident in their work, and not only in the time of the ancient Greeks, for the same can be said for Shakespearean and more recent works that have been widely called "tragic."

How do we know when we are in the presence of the tragic? Or, as Mason puts it, how do we recognize the tragic plane? Some years ago I ran across a passage in an essay by the philosopher Stanley Cavell that describes something I experience in great tragic works. The essay itself has nothing directly to do with tragedy; it describes Wittgenstein's method of philosophical inquiry. Cavell compares Wittgenstein's method to the process of psychoanalysis. "As in psychotherapy," Cavell writes, "problems are solved only when they disappear, and answers are arrived at only when there are no longer questions. . . . The more one learns the hang of one's self, and mounts one's problems, the less one is able to say what one has learned; not because you have *forgotten* what it was, but because nothing you say would seem like an answer or a solution: there is no longer any question or problem which your words would match. You have reached conviction, but not about a proposition; and consistency, but not in a theory. You are different, what you recognize as problems are different, your world is different" (p. 85).

That seems to me to describe the moment when Oedipus finally allows himself to know the identities of the man he killed, and of his own wife and children. The world has completely changed in an instant. Such is the moment in *Bakkhai* when Pentheus realizes that the young stranger he has bullied is unlike any being he has seen before. Such is the moment when Othello grasps the character of the woman he has killed and his own capacity for error. Such is the moment at the end of *The Winter's Tale* when Leontes discovers that the statue of his long-dead wife breathes. In a moment, the world has become an entirely different thing, so different that one can barely recall thinking of it differently from the way it has now come to seem.

Such is the moment when Josie discovers that Jim is completely un-like the man she thought she knew for twenty years. Such moments, for me, are touchstones by which I know I am probably in the presence of the tragic.

We know that O'Neill explicitly worked from ancient models during the 1920s, that the story of *Desire Under the Elms* closely follows the myth of Hippolytos and Euripides' play by that name. We know that O'Neill explicitly modeled his Electra trilogy on Aeschylus's *Oresteia,* and we find extended allusions to Greek myths and tragic drama in such plays as *The Emperor Jones, The Great God Brown, Strange Interlude, Dynamo,* and *Lazarus Laughed,* among others.

The capacity to create the condition in which conflicting ways of trying to perceive reality collide against each other seems fundamental to the power to make tragic art. Such a capacity seems more likely to occur in times of great changes in the ways we understand our lives, our world, and whatever connects us to life. The discovery that the world is nothing like it has seemed to be a moment before shows Oedipus to have learned *something,* at least, from his ordeal, although what he has learned is not what we might call today "empowering" but perhaps just the opposite. It shows that nothing he has done or known has taught him anything of value about the nature of life and the world. And so he goes into the wilderness without eyes and without any illusions that if he could see, sight would give him any control over his future.

I think this view of tragedy describes very well what O'Neill attempted to do in the 1920s, and that it shows very well how O'Neill's late plays work. At the end of *Long Day's Journey* Edmund seems to know at least as much as Oedipus knew at the end of his play. Living in the house of Tyrone has taught him only that he knows almost nothing and will somehow have to begin to learn. But that knowledge is not a small thing. At the end of *Moon* the audience knows that Josie has learned from Jim Tyrone's dreadful story that wherever her life is to go, she can no longer continue to be simply aide and audience to her father's schemes and jokes, and that the world is far different from what she has let herself know of it. First she must mourn. Then she may begin to learn.

REFERENCES AND SUGGESTIONS
FOR FURTHER READING

Barlow, Judith E., *Final Acts: The Creation of Three Late O'Neill Plays*. Athens: University of Georgia Press, 1985.

Black, Stephen A., *Eugene O'Neill, Beyond Mourning and Tragedy*. New Haven: Yale University Press, 1999.

———, *File on O'Neill*. London: Methuen, 1993.

———, "Letting the Dead Be Dead: A Reinterpretation of *A Moon for the Misbegotten*," *Modern Drama* 29 (1986): pp. 544–55.

Cavell, Stanley, *Must We Mean What We Say: A Book of Essays*. Cambridge: Cambridge University Press, 1969.

Floyd, Virginia, *Eugene O'Neill at Work*. New York: Frederick Ungar, 1981.

Lee, M. Owen, *Athena Sings: Wagner and the Greeks*. Toronto: University of Toronto Press, 2003.

Mason, H. A., *The Tragic Plane*. Oxford: Clarendon Press, 1985.

Shaeffer, Louis, *Eugene O'Neill: Son and Artist*. New York: Little, Brown, 1973.

———, *Eugene O'Neill: Son and Playwright*. New York: Little, Brown, 1968.

Voelker, Paul, "A Full *Moon* in Minneapolis." *The Eugene O'Neill Newsletter* 1, no. 3 (January 1978).

A Moon for the Misbegotten

# Scenes

*The play takes place in Connecticut at the home of tenant farmer,* PHIL
HOGAN, *between the hours of noon on a day in early September, 1923,
and sunrise of the following day.*

*The house is not, to speak mildly, a fine example of New England ar-
chitecture, placed so perfectly in its setting that it appears a harmonious
part of the landscape, rooted in the earth. It has been moved to its present
site, and looks it. An old boxlike, clapboarded affair, with a shingled
roof and brick chimney, it is propped up about two feet above ground by
layers of timber blocks. There are two windows on the lower floor of this
side of the house which faces front, and one window on the floor above.
These windows have no shutters, curtains or shades. Each has at least
one pane missing, a square of cardboard taking its place. The house had*

*once been painted a repulsive yellow with brown trim, but the walls now are a blackened and weathered gray, flaked with streaks and splotches of dim lemon. Just around the left corner of the house, a flight of steps leads to the front door.*

*To make matters worse, a one-story, one-room addition has been tacked on at right. About twelve feet long by six high, this room, which is* JOSIE HOGAN'S *bedroom, is evidently homemade. Its walls and sloping roof are covered with tar paper, faded to dark gray. Close to where it joins the house, there is a door with a flight of three unpainted steps leading to the ground. At right of door is a small window.*

*From these steps there is a footpath going around an old pear tree, at right-rear, through a field of hay stubble to a patch of woods. The same path also extends left to join a dirt road which leads up from the county highway (about a hundred yards off left) to the front door of the house, and thence back through a scraggly orchard of apple trees to the barn. Close to the house, under the window next to* JOSIE'S *bedroom, there is a big boulder with a flat top.*

# Act One

*As described. It is just before noon. The day is clear and hot.*

*The door of* JOSIE'*s bedroom opens and she comes out on the steps, bending to avoid bumping her head.*

JOSIE *is twenty-eight. She is so oversize for a woman that she is almost a freak—five feet eleven in her stockings and weighs around one hundred and eighty. Her sloping shoulders are broad, her chest deep with large, firm breasts, her waist wide but slender by contrast with her hips and thighs. She has long smooth arms, immensely strong, although no muscles show. The same is true of her legs.*

*She is more powerful than any but an exceptionally strong man, able to do the manual labor of two ordinary men. But there is no mannish quality about her. She is all woman.*

*The map of Ireland is stamped on her face, with its long upper lip and small nose, thick black eyebrows, black hair as coarse as a horse's mane, freckled, sunburned fair skin, high cheekbones and heavy jaw. It is not a pretty face, but her large dark-blue eyes give it a note of beauty, and her smile, revealing even white teeth, gives it charm.*

*She wears a cheap, sleeveless, blue cotton dress. Her feet are bare, the soles earth-stained and tough as leather.*

*She comes down the steps and goes left to the corner of the house and peers around it toward the barn. Then she moves swiftly to the right of the house and looks back.*

JOSIE

Ah, thank God.

*She goes back toward the steps as her brother,* MIKE, *appears hurrying up from right-rear.*

MIKE HOGAN *is twenty, about four inches shorter than his sister. He is sturdily built, but seems almost puny compared to her. He has a common Irish face, its expression sullen, or slyly cunning, or primly self-righteous. He never forgets that he is a good Catholic, faithful to all the observances, and so is one of the élite of Almighty God in a world of damned sinners composed of Protestants and bad Catholics. In brief,* MIKE *is a New England Irish Catholic Puritan, Grade B, and an extremely irritating youth to have around.*

MIKE *wears dirty overalls, a sweat-stained brown shirt. He carries a pitchfork.*

JOSIE

Bad luck to you for a slowpoke. Didn't I tell you half-past eleven?

MIKE

How could I sneak here sooner with him peeking round the corner of the barn to catch me if I took a minute's rest, the way he always does? I had to wait till he went to the pig pen.

*He adds viciously.*

Where he belongs, the old hog!

JOSIE'S *right arm strikes with surprising swiftness and her big hand lands on the side of his jaw. She means it to be only a slap, but his head jerks back and he stumbles, dropping the pitchfork, and pleads cringingly.*

Don't hit me, Josie! Don't, now!

JOSIE

*Quietly.*

Then keep your tongue off him. He's my father, too, and I like him, if you don't.

MIKE

*Out of her reach—sullenly.*

You're two of a kind, and a bad kind.

6

JOSIE

*Good-naturedly.*

I'm proud of it. And I didn't hit you, or you'd be flat on the ground.
It was only a love tap to waken your wits, so you'll use them. If he
catches you running away, he'll beat you half to death. Get your bag
now. I've packed it. It's inside the door of my room with your coat
laid over it. Hurry now, while I see what he's doing.

*She moves quickly to peer around the corner of the house at left. He goes
up the steps into her room and returns carrying an old coat and a cheap
bulging satchel. She comes back.*

There's no sight of him.

MIKE *drops the satchel on the ground while he puts on the coat.*

I put everything in the bag. You can change to your Sunday suit in
the can at the station or in the train, and don't forget to wash your
face. I know you want to look your best when our brother, Thomas,
sees you on his doorstep.

*Her tone becomes derisively amused.*

And him way up in the world, a noble sergeant of the Bridgeport
police. Maybe he'll get you on the force. It'd suit you. I can see you
leading drunks to the lockup while you give them a lecture on temperance. Or if Thomas can't get you a job, he'll pass you along to
our brother, John, the noble barkeep in Meriden. He'll teach you
the trade. You'll make a nice one, who'll never steal from the till, or
drink, and who'll tell customers they've had enough and better go
home just when they're beginning to feel happy.

*She sighs regretfully.*

Ah, well, Mike, you was born a priest's pet, and there's no help for it.

MIKE

That's right! Make fun of me again, because I want to be decent.

JOSIE

You're worse than decent. You're virtuous.

MIKE

Well, that's a thing nobody can say about—

*He stops, a bit ashamed, but mostly afraid to finish.*

7

JOSIE
*Amused.*
About me? No, and what's more, they don't.
*She smiles mockingly.*
I know what a trial it's been to you, Mike, having a sister who's the scandal of the neighborhood.

MIKE
It's you that's saying it, not me. I don't want to part with hard feelings. And I'll keep on praying for you.

JOSIE
*Roughly.*
Och! To hell with your prayers!

MIKE
*Stiffly.*
I'm going.
*He picks up his bag.*

JOSIE
*Her manner softening.*
Wait.
*She comes to him.*
Don't mind my rough tongue, Mike. I'm sorry to see you go, but it's the best thing for you. That's why I'm helping you, the same as I helped Thomas and John. You can't stand up to the Old Man any more than Thomas or John could, and the old divil would always keep you a slave. I wish you all the luck in the world, Mike. I know you'll get on—and God bless you.
*Her voice has softened, and she blinks back tears. She kisses him—then fumbling in the pocket of her dress, pulls out a little roll of one-dollar bills and presses it in his hand.*
Here's a little present over your fare. I took it from his little green bag, and won't he be wild when he finds out! But I can handle him.

MIKE
*Enviously.*
You can. You're the only one.

*Gratefully moved for a second.*
Thank you, Josie. You've a kind heart.
*Then virtuously.*
But I don't like taking stolen money.

JOSIE

Don't be a bigger jackass than you are already. Tell your conscience it's a bit of the wages he's never given you.

MIKE

That's true, Josie. It's rightfully mine.
*He shoves the money into his pocket.*

JOSIE

Get along now, so you won't miss the trolley. And don't forget to get off the train at Bridgeport. Give my love to Thomas and John. No, never mind. They've not written me in years. Give them a boot in the tail for me.

MIKE

That's nice talk for a woman. You've a tongue as dirty as the Old Man's.

JOSIE

*Impatiently.*
Don't start preaching, like you love to, or you'll never go.

MIKE

You're as bad as he is, almost. It's his influence made you what you are, and him always scheming how he'll cheat people, selling them a broken-down nag or a sick cow or pig that he's doctored up to look good for a day or two. It's no better than stealing, and you help him.

JOSIE

I do. Sure, it's grand fun.

MIKE

You ought to marry and have a home of your own away from this shanty and stop your shameless ways with men.
*He adds, not without moral satisfaction.*
Though it'd be hard to find a decent man who'd have you now.

JOSIE

I don't want a decent man, thank you. They're no fun. They're all
sticks like you. And I wouldn't marry the best man on earth and be
tied down to him alone.

MIKE

*With a cunning leer.*
Not even Jim Tyrone, I suppose?
*She stares at him.*
You'd like being tied to money, I know that, and he'll be rich when
his mother's estate is settled.
*Sarcastically.*
I suppose you've never thought of that? Don't tell me! I've watched
you making sheep's eyes at him.

JOSIE

*Contemptuously.*
So I'm leading Jim on to propose, am I?

MIKE

I know it's crazy, but maybe you're hoping if you got hold of him
alone when he's mad drunk— Anyway, talk all you please to put me
off, I'll bet my last penny you've cooked up some scheme to hook
him, and the Old Man put you up to it. Maybe he thinks if he caught
you with Jim and had witnesses to prove it, and his shotgun to scare
him—

JOSIE

*Controlling her anger.*
You're full of bright thoughts. I wouldn't strain my brains any more,
if I was you.

MIKE

Well, I wouldn't put it past the Old Man to try any trick. And I
wouldn't put it past you, God forgive you. You've never cared about
your virtue, or what man you went out with. You've always been brazen as brass and proud of your disgrace. You can't deny that, Josie.

JOSIE

I don't.

*Then ominously.*

You'd better shut up now. I've been holding my temper, because we're saying good-bye.

*She stands up.*

But I'm losing patience.

MIKE

*Hastily.*

Wait till I finish and you won't be mad at me. I was going to say I wish you luck with your scheming, for once. I hate Jim Tyrone's guts, with his quotin' Latin and his high-toned Jesuit College education, putting on airs as if he was too good to wipe his shoes on me, when he's nothing but a drunken bum who never done a tap of work in his life, except acting on the stage while his father was alive to get him the jobs.

*Vindictively.*

I'll pray you'll find a way to nab him, Josie, and skin him out of his last nickel!

JOSIE

*Makes a threatening move toward him.*

One more word out of you—

*Then contemptuously.*

You're a dirty tick and it'd serve you right if I let you stay gabbing until Father came and beat you to a jelly, but I won't. I'm too anxious to be rid of you.

*Roughly.*

Get out of here, now! Do you think he'll stay all day with the pigs, you gabbing fool?

*She goes left to peer around the corner of the house—with real alarm.*

There he is, coming up to the barn.

MIKE *grabs the satchel, terrified. He slinks swiftly around the corner and disappears along the path to the woods, right-rear. She keeps watching her father and does not notice* MIKE'S *departure.*

He's looking toward the meadow. He sees you're not working. He's running down there. He'll come here next. You'd better run for your life!

*She turns and sees he's gone—contemptuously.*

I might have known. I'll bet you're a mile away by now, you rabbit!

*She peeks around the corner again—with amused admiration.*

Look at my poor old father pelt. He's as spry on his stumpy legs as a yearling—and as full of rage as a nest of wasps!

*She laughs and comes back to look along the path to the woods.*

Well, that's the last of you, Mike, and good riddance. It was the little boy you used to be that I had to mother, and not you, I stole the money for.

*This dismisses him. She sighs.*

Well, himself will be here in a minute. I'd better be ready.

*She reaches in her bedroom corner by the door and takes out a sawed-off broom handle.*

Not that I need it, but it saves his pride.

*She sits on the steps with the broom handle propped against the steps near her right hand. A moment later, her father,* PHIL HOGAN, *comes running up from left-rear and charges around the corner of the house, his arms pumping up and down, his fists clenched, his face full of fighting fury.*

HOGAN *is fifty-five, about five feet six. He has a thick neck, lumpy, sloping shoulders, a barrel-like trunk, stumpy legs, and big feet. His arms are short and muscular, with large hairy hands. His head is round with thinning sandy hair. His face is fat with a snub nose, long upper lip, big mouth, and little blue eyes with bleached lashes and eyebrows that remind one of a white pig's. He wears heavy brogans, filthy overalls, and a dirty short-sleeved undershirt. Arms and face are sunburned and freckled. On his head is an old wide-brimmed hat of coarse straw that would look more becoming on a horse. His voice is high-pitched with a pronounced brogue.*

HOGAN

*Stops as he turns the corner and sees her—furiously.*

Where is he? Is he hiding in the house? I'll wipe the floors with him, the lazy bastard!

*Turning his anger against her.*

Haven't you a tongue in your head, you great slut you?

12

JOSIE

*With provoking calm.*

Don't be calling me names, you bad-tempered old hornet, or maybe I'll lose my temper, too.

HOGAN

To hell with your temper, you overgrown cow!

JOSIE

I'd rather be a cow than an ugly little buck goat. You'd better sit down and cool off. Old men shouldn't run around raging in the noon sun. You'll get sunstroke.

HOGAN

To hell with sunstroke! Have you seen him?

JOSIE

Have I seen who?

HOGAN

Mike! Who else would I be after, the Pope? He was in the meadow, but the minute I turned my back he sneaked off.

*He sees the pitchfork.*

There's his pitchfork! Will you stop your lying!

JOSIE

I haven't said I didn't see him.

HOGAN

Then don't try to help him hide from me, or— Where is he?

JOSIE

Where you'll never find him.

HOGAN

We'll soon see! I'll bet he's in your room under the bed, the cowardly lump!

*He moves toward the steps.*

JOSIE

He's not. He's gone like Thomas and John before him to escape your slave-driving.

HOGAN

*Stares at her incredulously.*

You mean he's run off to make his own way in the world?

JOSIE

He has. So make up your mind to it, and sit down.

HOGAN

*Baffled, sits on the boulder and takes off his hat to scratch his head—
with a faint trace of grudging respect.*

I'd never dream he had that much spunk.

*His temper rising again.*

And I know damned well he hadn't, not without you to give him the
guts and help him, like the great soft fool you are!

JOSIE

Now don't start raging again, Father.

HOGAN

*Seething.*

You've stolen my satchel to give him, I suppose, like you did before
for Thomas and John?

JOSIE

It was my satchel, too. Didn't I help you in the trade for the horse,
when you got the Crowleys to throw in the satchel for good mea-
sure? I was up all night fixing that nag's forelegs so his knees wouldn't
buckle together till after the Crowleys had him a day or two.

HOGAN

*Forgets his anger to grin reminiscently.*

You've a wonderful way with animals, God bless you. And do you
remember the two Crowleys came back to give me a beating, and I
licked them both?

JOSIE

*With calculating flattery.*

You did. You're a wonderful fighter. Sure, you could give Jack Demp-
sey himself a run for his money.

HOGAN

*With sharp suspicion.*

I could, but don't try to change the subject and fill me with blarney.

JOSIE

All right. I'll tell the truth then. They were getting the best of you till I ran out and knocked one of them tail over tin cup against the pigpen.

HOGAN

*Outraged.*

You're a liar! They was begging for mercy before you came.

*Furiously.*

You thief, you! You stole my fine satchel for that lump! And I'll bet that's not all. I'll bet, like when Thomas and John sneaked off, you—

*He rises from the boulder threateningly.*

Listen, Josie, if you found where I hid my little green bag, and stole my money to give to that lousy altar boy, I'll—

JOSIE

*Rises from the steps with the broom handle in her right hand.*

Well, I did. So now what'll you do? Don't be threatening me. You know I'll beat better sense in your skull if you lay a finger on me.

HOGAN

I never yet laid hands on a woman—not when I was sober—but if it wasn't for that club—

*Bitterly.*

A fine curse God put on me when he gave me a daughter as big and strong as a bull, and as vicious and disrespectful.

*Suddenly his eyes twinkle and he grins admiringly.*

Be God, look at you standing there with the club! If you ain't the damnedest daughter in Connecticut, who is?

*He chuckles and sits on the boulder again.*

JOSIE

*Laughs and sits on the steps, putting the club away.*

And if you ain't the damnedest father in Connecticut, who is?

HOGAN
*Takes a clay pipe and plug of tobacco and knife from his pocket. He cuts
the plug and stuffs his pipe—without rancor.*
How much did you steal, Josie?

JOSIE
Six dollars only.

HOGAN
*Only!* Well, God grant someone with wits will see that dopey gander
at the depot and sell him the railroad for the six.
*Grumbling.*
It isn't the money I mind, Josie—

JOSIE
I know. Sure, what do you care for money? You'd give your last penny
to the first beggar you met—if he had a shotgun pointed at your
heart!

HOGAN
Don't be teasing. You know what I mean. It's the thought of that
pious lump having my money that maddens me. I wouldn't put it
past him to drop it in the collection plate next Sunday, he's that big
a jackass.

JOSIE
I knew when you'd calmed down you'd think it worth six dollars to
see the last of him.

HOGAN
*Finishes filling his pipe.*
Well, maybe I do. To tell the truth, I never liked him.
*He strikes a match on the seat of his overalls and lights his pipe.*
And I never liked Thomas and John, either.

JOSIE
*Amused.*
You've the same bad luck in sons I have in brothers.

HOGAN
*Puffs ruminatively.*

They all take after your mother's family. She was the only one in it had spirit, God rest her soul. The rest of them was a pious lousy lot. They wouldn't dare put food in their mouths before they said grace for it. They was too busy preaching temperance to have time for a drink. They spent so much time confessing their sins, they had no chance to do any sinning.

*He spits disgustedly.*

The scum of the earth! Thank God, you're like me and your mother.

JOSIE

I don't know if I should thank God for being like you. Sure, everyone says you're a wicked old tick, as crooked as a corkscrew.

HOGAN

I know. They're an envious lot, God forgive them.

*They both chuckle. He pulls on his pipe reflectively.*

You didn't get much thanks from Mike, I'll wager, for your help.

JOSIE

Oh, he thanked me kindly. And then he started to preach about my sins — and yours.

HOGAN

Oho, did he?

*Exploding.*

For the love of God, why didn't you hold him till I could give him one good kick for a father's parting blessing!

JOSIE

I near gave him one myself.

HOGAN

When I think your poor mother was killed bringing that crummy calf into life!

*Vindictively.*

I've never set foot in a church since, and never will.

*A pause. He speaks with a surprising sad gentleness.*

A sweet woman. Do you remember her, Josie? You were only a little thing when she died.

JOSIE

I remember her well.

*With a teasing smile which is half sad.*

She was the one could put you in your place when you'd come home drunk and want to tear down the house for the fun of it.

HOGAN

*With admiring appreciation.*

Yes, she could do it, God bless her. I only raised my hand to her once—just a slap because she told me to stop singing, it was after daylight. The next moment I was on the floor thinking a mule had kicked me.

*He chuckles.*

Since you've grown up, I've had the same trouble. There's no liberty in my own home.

JOSIE

That's lucky—or there wouldn't be any home.

HOGAN

*After a pause of puffing on his pipe.*

What did that donkey, Mike, preach to you about?

JOSIE

Oh, the same as ever—that I'm the scandal of the countryside, carrying on with men without a marriage license.

HOGAN

*Gives her a strange, embarrassed glance and then looks away. He does not look at her during the following dialogue. His manner is casual.*

Hell roast his soul for saying it. But it's true enough.

JOSIE

*Defiantly.*

It is, and what of it? I don't care a damn for the scandal.

HOGAN

No. You do as you please and to hell with everyone.

**JOSIE**

Yes, and that goes for you, too, if you are my father. So don't you start preaching too.

**HOGAN**

Me, preach? Sure, the divil would die laughing. Don't bring me into it. I learned long since to let you go your own way because there's no controlling you.

**JOSIE**

I do my work and I earn my keep and I've a right to be free.

**HOGAN**

You have. I've never denied it.

**JOSIE**

No. You've never. I've often wondered why a man that likes fights as much as you didn't grab at the excuse of my disgrace to beat the lights out of the men.

**HOGAN**

Wouldn't I look a great fool, when everyone knows any man who tried to make free with you, and you not willing, would be carried off to the hospital? Anyway, I wouldn't want to fight an army. You've had too many sweethearts.

**JOSIE**

*With a proud toss of her head—boastfully.*
That's because I soon get tired of any man and give him his walking papers.

**HOGAN**

I'm afraid you were born to be a terrible wanton woman. But to tell the truth, I'm well satisfied you're what you are, though I shouldn't say it, because if you was the decent kind, you'd have married some fool long ago, and I'd have lost your company and your help on the farm.

**JOSIE**

*With a trace of bitterness.*
Leave it to you to think of your own interest.

HOGAN
*Puffs on his pipe.*
What else did my beautiful son, Mike, say to you?

JOSIE
Oh, he was full of stupid gab, as usual. He gave me good advice—

HOGAN
*Grimly.*
That was kind of him. It must have been good—

JOSIE
I ought to marry and settle down—if I could find a decent man who'd have me, which he was sure I couldn't.

HOGAN
*Beginning to boil.*
I tell you, Josie, it's going to be the saddest memory of my life I didn't get one last swipe at him!

JOSIE
So the only hope, he thought, was for me to catch some indecent man, who'd have money coming to him I could steal.

HOGAN
*Gives her a quick, probing side glance—casually.*
He meant Jim Tyrone?

JOSIE
He did. And the dirty tick accused you and me of making up a foxy scheme to trap Jim. I'm to get him alone when he's crazy drunk and lead him on to marry me.
*She adds in a hard, scornful tone.*
As if that would ever work. Sure, all the pretty little tarts on Broadway, New York, must have had a try at that, and much good it did them.

HOGAN
*Again with a quick side glance—casually.*
They must have, surely. But that's in the city where he's suspicious. You never can tell what he mightn't do here in the country, where

he's innocent, with a moon in the sky to fill him with poetry and a quart of bad hootch inside of him.

JOSIE
*Turns on him angrily.*
Are you taking Mike's scheme seriously, you old goat?

HOGAN
I'm not. I only thought you wanted my opinion.
*She regards him suspiciously, but his face is blank, as if he hadn't a thought beyond enjoying his pipe.*

JOSIE
*Turning away.*
And if that didn't work, Mike said maybe we had a scheme that I'd get Jim in bed with me and you'd come with witnesses and a shot-gun, and catch him there.

HOGAN
Faith, me darlin' son never learnt that from his prayer book! He must have improved his mind on the sly.

JOSIE
The dirty tick!

HOGAN
Don't call him a tick. I don't like ticks but I'll say this for them, I never picked one off me yet was a hypocrite.

JOSIE
Him daring to accuse us of planning a rotten trick like that on Jim!

HOGAN
*As if he misunderstood her meaning.*
Yes, it's as old as the hills. Everyone's heard of it. But it still works now and again, I'm told, and sometimes an old trick is best because it's so ancient no one would suspect you'd try it.

JOSIE
*Staring at him resentfully.*
That's enough out of you, Father. I never can tell to this day, when

you put that dead mug on you, whether you're joking or not, but I don't want to hear any more—

HOGAN
*Mildly.*
I thought you wanted my honest opinion on the merits of Mike's suggestion.

JOSIE
Och, shut up, will you? I know you're only trying to make game of me. You like Jim and you'd never play a dirty trick on him, not even if I was willing.

HOGAN
No—not unless I found he was playing one on me.

JOSIE
Which he'd never.

HOGAN
No, I wouldn't think it, but my motto in life is never trust anyone too far, not even myself.

JOSIE
You've reason for the last. I've often suspected you sneak out of bed in the night to pick your own pockets.

HOGAN
I wouldn't call it a dirty trick on him to get you for a wife.

JOSIE
*Exasperatedly.*
God save us, are you off on that again?

HOGAN
Well, you've put marriage in my head and I can't help considering the merits of the case, as they say. Sure, you're two of a kind, both great disgraces. That would help make a happy marriage because neither of you could look down on the other.

JOSIE
Jim mightn't think so.

HOGAN

You mean he'd think he was marrying beneath his station? He'd be a damned fool if he had that notion, for his Old Man who'd worked up from nothing to be rich and famous didn't give a damn about station. Didn't I often see him working on his grounds in clothes I wouldn't put on a scarecrow, not caring who saw him?
*With admiring affection.*
God rest him, he was a true Irish gentleman.

JOSIE

He was, and didn't you swindle him, and make me help you at it? I remember when I was a slip of a girl, and you'd get a letter saying his agent told him you were a year behind in the rent, and he'd be damned if he'd stand for it, and he was coming here to settle the matter. You'd make me dress up, with my hair brushed and a ribbon in it, and leave me to soften his heart before he saw you. So I'd skip down the path to meet him, and make him a courtesy, and hold on to his hand, and bat my eyes at him and lead him in the house, and offer him a drink of the good whiskey you didn't keep for company, and gape at him and tell him he was the handsomest man in the world, and the fierce expression he'd put on for you would go away.

HOGAN
*Chuckles.*
You did it wonderful. You should have gone on the stage.

JOSIE
*Dryly.*
Yes, that's what he'd tell me, and he'd reach in his pocket and take out a half dollar, and ask me if you hadn't put me up to it. So I'd say yes, you had.

HOGAN
*Sadly.*
I never knew you were such a black traitor, and you only a child.

JOSIE
And then you'd come and before he could get a word out of him,

you'd tell him you'd vacate the premises unless he lowered the rent and painted the house.

HOGAN
Be God, that used to stop him in his tracks.

JOSIE
It didn't stop him from saying you were the damnedest crook ever came out of Ireland.

HOGAN
He said it with admiration. And we'd start drinking and telling stories, and singing songs, and by the time he left we were both too busy cursing England to worry over the rent.
*He grins affectionately.*
Oh, he was a great man entirely.

JOSIE
He was. He always saw through your tricks.

HOGAN
Didn't I know he would? Sure, all I wanted was to give him the fun of seeing through them so he couldn't be hard-hearted. That was the real trick.

JOSIE
*Stares at him.*
You old divil, you've always a trick hidden behind your tricks, so no one can tell at times what you're after.

HOGAN
Don't be so suspicious. Sure, I'd never try to fool you. You know me too well. But we've gone off the track. It's Jim we're discussing, not his father. I was telling you I could see the merit in your marrying him.

JOSIE
*Exasperatedly.*
Och, a cow must have kicked you in the head this morning.

HOGAN

I'd never give it a thought if I didn't know you had a soft spot in your heart for him.

JOSIE

*Resentfully.*

Well, I haven't! I like him, if that's what you mean, but it's only to talk to, because he's educated and quiet-spoken and has politeness even when he's drunkest, and doesn't roar around cursing and singing, like some I could name.

HOGAN

If you could see the light in your eyes when he blarneys you—

JOSIE

*Roughly.*

The light in me foot!

*Scornfully.*

I'm in love with him, you'll be saying next!

HOGAN

*Ignores this.*

And another merit of the case is, he likes you.

JOSIE

Because he keeps dropping in here lately? Sure, it's only when he gets sick of the drunks at the Inn, and it's more to joke with you than see me.

HOGAN

It's your happiness I'm considering when I recommend your using your wits to catch him, if you can.

JOSIE

*Jeeringly.*

If!

HOGAN

Who knows? With all the sweethearts you've had, you must have a catching way with men.

JOSIE

*Boastfully.*

Maybe I have. But that doesn't mean—

HOGAN

If you got him alone tonight—there'll be a beautiful moon to fill him with poetry and loneliness, and—

JOSIE

That's one of Mike's dirty schemes.

HOGAN

Mike be damned! Sure, that's every woman's scheme since the world was created. Without it there'd be no population.

*Persuasively.*

There'd be no harm trying it, anyway.

JOSIE

And no use, either.

*Bitterly.*

Och, Father, don't play the jackass with me. You know, and I know, I'm an ugly overgrown lump of a woman, and the men that want me are no better than stupid bulls. Jim can have all the pretty, painted little Broadway girls he wants—and dancers on the stage, too—when he comes into his estate. That's the kind he likes.

HOGAN

I notice he's never married one. Maybe he'd like a fine strong handsome figure of a woman for a change, with beautiful eyes and hair and teeth and a smile.

JOSIE

*Pleased, but jeering.*

Thank you kindly for your compliments. Now I know a cow kicked you in the head.

HOGAN

If you think Jim hasn't been taking in your fine points, you're a fool.

JOSIE

You mean you've noticed him?

*Suddenly furious.*
Stop your lying!

HOGAN

Don't fly in a temper. All I'm saying is, there may be a chance in it to better yourself.

JOSIE
*Scornfully.*
Better myself by being tied down to a man who's drunk every night of his life? No, thank you!

HOGAN

Sure, you're strong enough to reform him. A taste of that club you've got, when he came home to you paralyzed, and in a few weeks you'd have him a dirty prohibitionist.

JOSIE
*Seriously.*
It's true, if I was his wife, I'd cure him of drinking himself to death, if I had to kill him.
*Then angrily.*
Och, I'm sick of your crazy gab, Father! Leave me alone!

HOGAN

Well, let's put it another way. Don't tell me you couldn't learn to love the estate he'll come into.

JOSIE
*Resentfully.*
Ah, I've been waiting for that. That's what Mike said, again. Now we've come to the truth behind all your blather of my liking him or him liking me.
*Her manner changing—defiantly.*
All right, then. Of course I'd love the money. Who wouldn't? And why shouldn't I get my hands on it, if I could? He's bound to be swindled out of it, anyway. He'll go back to the Broadway he thinks is heaven, and by the time the pretty little tarts, and the barroom sponges and racetrack touts and gamblers are through with him he'll

be picked clean. I'm no saint, God knows, but I'm decent and deserving compared to those scum.

HOGAN
*Eagerly.*
Be God, now you're using your wits. And where there's a will there's a way. You and me have never been beat when we put our brains together. I'll keep thinking it over, and you do the same.

JOSIE
*With illogical anger.*
Well, I won't! And you keep your mad scheming to yourself. I won't listen to it.

HOGAN
*As if he were angry, too.*
All right. The divil take you. It's all you'll hear from me.
*He pauses—then with great seriousness, turning toward her.*
Except one thing—
*As she starts to shut him up—sharply.*
I'm serious, and you'd better listen, because it's about this farm, which is home to us.

JOSIE
*Surprised, stares at him.*
What about the farm?

HOGAN
Don't forget, if we have lived on it twenty years, we're only tenants and we could be thrown out on our necks any time.
*Quickly.*
Mind you, I don't say Jim would ever do it, rent or no rent, or let the executors do it, even if they wanted, which they don't, knowing they'd never find another tenant.

JOSIE
What's worrying you, then?

HOGAN

This. I've been afraid lately the minute the estate is out of probate, Jim will sell the farm.

JOSIE

*Exasperatedly.*

Of course he will! Hasn't he told us and promised you can buy it on easy time payments at the small price you offered?

HOGAN

Jim promises whatever you like when he's full of whiskey. He might forget a promise as easy when he's drunk enough.

JOSIE

*Indignantly.*

He'd never! And who'd want it except us? No one ever has in all the years—

HOGAN

Someone has lately. The agent got an offer last month, Jim told me, bigger than mine.

JOSIE

Och, Jim loves to try and get your goat. He was kidding you.

HOGAN

He wasn't. I can tell. He said he told the agent to tell whoever it was the place wasn't for sale.

JOSIE

Of course he did. Did he say who'd made the offer?

HOGAN

He didn't know. It came through a real-estate man who wouldn't tell who his client was. I've been trying to guess, but I can't think of anyone crazy enough unless it'd be some damn fool of a millionaire buying up land to make a great estate for himself, like our beautiful neighbor, Harder, the Standard Oil thief, did years ago.

*He adds with bitter fervency.*

May he roast in hell and his Limey superintendent with him!

JOSIE

Amen to that.

*Then scornfully.*

This land for an estate? And if there was an offer, Jim's refused it, and that ends it. He wouldn't listen to any offer, after he's given his word to us.

HOGAN

Did I say he would—when he's in his right mind? What I'm afraid of is, he might be led into it sometime when he has one of his sneering bitter drunks on and talks like a Broadway crook himself, saying money is the only thing in the world, and everything and anyone can be bought if the price is big enough. You've heard him.

JOSIE

I have. But he doesn't fool me at all. He only acts like he's hard and shameless to get back at life when it's tormenting him—and who doesn't?

*He gives her a quick, curious side glance which she doesn't notice.*

HOGAN

Or take the other kind of queer drunk he gets on sometimes when, without any reason you can see, he'll suddenly turn strange, and look sad, and stare at nothing as if he was mourning over some ghost inside him, and—

JOSIE

I think I know what comes over him when he's like that. It's the memory of his mother comes back and his grief for her death.

*Pityingly.*

Poor Jim.

HOGAN

*Ignoring this.*

And whiskey seems to have no effect on him, like water off a duck's back. He'll keep acting natural enough, and you'd swear he wasn't bad at all, but the next day you find his brain was so paralyzed he don't remember a thing until you remind him. He's done a lot of mad things, when he was that way, he was sorry for after.

JOSIE
*Scornfully.*
What drunk hasn't? But he'd never—
*Resentfully.*
I won't have you suspecting Jim without any cause, d'you hear me!

HOGAN
I don't suspect him. All I've said is, when a man gets as queer drunk as Jim, he doesn't know himself what he mightn't do, and we'd be damned fools if we didn't fear the possibility, however small it is, and do all we can to guard against it.

JOSIE
There's no possibility! And how could we guard against it, if there was?

HOGAN
Well, you can put yourself out to be extra nice to him, for one thing.

JOSIE
How nice is extra nice?

HOGAN
You ought to know. But here's one tip. I've noticed when you talk rough and brazen like you do to other men, he may grin like they do, as if he enjoyed it, but he don't. So watch your tongue.

JOSIE
*With a defiant toss of her head.*
I'll talk as I please, and if he don't like it he can lump it!
*Scornfully.*
I'm to pretend I'm a pure virgin, I suppose? That would fool him, wouldn't it, and him hearing all about me from the men at the Inn?
*She gets to her feet, abruptly changing the subject.*
We're wasting the day, blathering.
*Then her face hardening.*
If he ever went back on his word, no matter how drunk he was, I'd be with you in any scheme you made against him, no matter how dirty.
*Hastily.*

31

But it's all your nonsense. I'd never believe it.
*She comes and picks up the pitchfork.*
I'll go to the meadow and finish Mike's work. You needn't fear you'll miss his help on the farm.

HOGAN

A hell of a help! A weak lazy back and the appetite of a drove of starving pigs!
*As she turns to go — suddenly bellicose.*
Leaving me, are you? When it's dinner time? Where's my dinner, you lazy cow?

JOSIE

There's stew on the stove, you bad-tempered runt. Go in and help yourself. I'm not hungry. Your gab has bothered my mind. I need hard work in the sun to clear it.
*She starts to go off toward rear-right.*

HOGAN

*Glancing down the road, off left-front.*
You'd better wait. There's a caller coming to the gate — and if I'm not mistaken, it's the light of your eyes himself.

JOSIE

*Angrily.*
Shut up!
*She stares off — her face softens and grows pitying.*
Look at him when he thinks no one is watching, with his eyes on the ground. Like a dead man walking slow behind his own coffin.
*Then roughly.*
Faith, he must have a hangover. He sees us now. Look at the bluff he puts up, straightening himself and grinning.
*Resentfully.*
I don't want to meet him. Let him make jokes with you and play the old game about a drink you both think is such fun. That's all he comes for, anyway.
*She starts off again.*

HOGAN

Are you running away from him? Sure, you must be afraid you're in love.

JOSIE *halts instantly and turns back defiantly. He goes on.*

Go in the house now, and wash your face, and tidy your dress, and give a touch to your hair. You want to look decent for him.

JOSIE

*Angrily.*

I'll go in the house, but only to see the stew ain't burned, for I suppose you'll have the foxiness to ask him to have a bite to eat to keep in his good graces.

HOGAN

Why shouldn't I ask him? I know damned well he has no appetite this early in the day, but only a thirst.

JOSIE

Och, you make me sick, you sly miser!

*She goes in through her bedroom, slamming the door behind her.* HOGAN *refills his pipe, pretending he doesn't notice* TYRONE *approaching, his eyes bright with droll expectation.* JIM TYRONE *enters along the road from the highway, left.*

TYRONE *is in his early forties, around five feet nine, broad-shouldered and deep-chested. His naturally fine physique has become soft and soggy from dissipation, but his face is still good-looking despite its unhealthy puffiness and the bags under the eyes. He has thinning dark hair, parted and brushed back to cover a bald spot. His eyes are brown, the whites congested and yellowish. His nose, big and aquiline, gives his face a certain Mephistophelian quality which is accentuated by his habitually cynical expression. But when he smiles without sneering, he still has the ghost of a former youthful, irresponsible Irish charm—that of the beguiling ne'er-do-well, sentimental and romantic. It is his humor and charm which have kept him attractive to women, and popular with men as a drinking companion. He is dressed in an expensive dark-brown suit, tight-fitting and drawn in at the waist, dark-brown made-to-order shoes and silk socks, a white silk shirt, silk handkerchief in breast pocket, a dark tie.*

*This get-up suggests that he follows a style set by well-groomed Broadway gamblers who would like to be mistaken for Wall Street brokers.*

*He has had enough pick-me-ups to recover from morning-after nausea and steady his nerves. During the following dialogue, he and* HOGAN *are like players at an old familiar game where each knows the other's moves, but which still amuses them.*

TYRONE

*Approaches and stands regarding* HOGAN *with sardonic relish.* HOGAN *scratches a match on the seat of his overalls and lights his pipe, pretending not to see him.* TYRONE *recites with feeling.*

"Fortunate senex, ergo tua rura manebunt,
    et tibi magna satis, quamvis lapis omnia nudus."

HOGAN

*Mutters.*

It's the landlord again, and my shotgun not handy.

*He looks up at* TYRONE.

Is it Mass you're saying, Jim? That was Latin. I know it by ear. What the hell—insult does it mean?

TYRONE

Translated very freely into Irish English, something like this.

*He imitates* HOGAN'S *brogue.*

"Ain't you the lucky old bastard to have this beautiful farm, if it is full of nude rocks."

HOGAN

I like that part about the rocks. If cows could eat them this place would make a grand dairy farm.

*He spits.*

It's easy to see you've a fine college education. It must be a big help to you, conversing with whores and barkeeps.

TYRONE

Yes, a very valuable worldly asset. I was once offered a job as office boy—until they discovered I wasn't qualified because I had no Bachelor of Arts diploma. There had been a slight misunderstanding just before I was to graduate.

HOGAN

Between you and the Fathers? I'll wager!

TYRONE

I made a bet with another Senior I could get a tart from the Haymarket to visit me, introduce her to the Jebs as my sister—and get away with it.

HOGAN

But you didn't?

TYRONE

Almost. It was a memorable day in the halls of learning. All the students were wise and I had them rolling in the aisles as I showed Sister around the grounds, accompanied by one of the Jebs. He was a bit suspicious at first, but Dutch Maisie—her professional name—had no make-up on, and was dressed in black, and had eaten a pound of Sen-Sen to kill the gin on her breath, and seemed such a devout girl that he forgot his suspicions.
*He pauses.*
Yes, all would have been well, but she was a mischievous minx, and had her own ideas of improving on my joke. When she was saying good-bye to Father Fuller, she added innocently: "Christ, Father, it's nice and quiet out here away from the damned Sixth Avenue El. I wish to hell I could stay here!"
*Dryly.*
But she didn't, and neither did I.

HOGAN

*Chuckles delightedly.*
I'll bet you didn't! God bless Dutch Maisie! I'd like to have known her.

TYRONE

*Sits down on the steps—with a change of manner.*
Well, how's the Duke of Donegal this fine day?

HOGAN

Never better.

TYRONE

Slaving and toiling as usual, I see.

HOGAN

Hasn't a poor man a right to his noon rest without being sneered at by his rich landlord?

TYRONE

"Rich" is good. I would be, if you'd pay up your back rent.

HOGAN

You ought to pay me, instead, for occupying this rockpile, miscalled a farm.
*His eyes twinkling.*
But I have fine reports to give you of a promising harvest. The milkweed and the thistles is in thriving condition, and I never saw the poison ivy so bounteous and beautiful.
TYRONE *laughs. Without their noticing,* JOSIE *appears in the doorway behind* TYRONE. *She has tidied up and arranged her hair. She smiles down at* JIM, *her face softening, pleased to hear him laugh.*

TYRONE

You win. Where did Josie go, Phil? I saw her here—

HOGAN

She ran in the house to make herself beautiful for you.

JOSIE

*Breaks in roughly.*
You're a liar.
*To* TYRONE, *her manner one of bold, free-and-easy familiarity.*
Hello, Jim.

TYRONE

*Starts to stand up.*
Hello, Josie.

JOSIE

*Puts a hand on his shoulder and pushes him down.*
Don't get up. Sure, you know I'm no lady.
*She sits on the top step—banteringly.*

36

How's my fine Jim this beautiful day? You don't look so bad. You must have stopped at the Inn for an eye-opener—or ten of them.

TYRONE

I've felt worse.

*He looks up at her sardonically.*

And how's my Virgin Queen of Ireland?

JOSIE

Yours, is it? Since when? And don't be miscalling me a virgin. You'll ruin my reputation, if you spread that lie about me.

*She laughs.* TYRONE *is staring at her. She goes on quickly.*

How is it you're around so early? I thought you never got up till afternoon.

TYRONE

Couldn't sleep. One of those heebie-jeebie nights when the booze keeps you awake instead of—

*He catches her giving him a pitying look—irritably.*

But what of it!

JOSIE

Maybe you had no woman in bed with you, for a change. It's a terrible thing to break the habit of years.

TYRONE

*Shrugs his shoulders.*

Maybe.

JOSIE

What's the matter with the tarts in town, they let you do it? I'll bet the ones you know on Broadway, New York, wouldn't neglect their business.

TYRONE

*Pretends to yawn boredly.*

Maybe not.

*Then irritably.*

Cut out the kidding, Josie. It's too early.

HOGAN
*Who has been taking everything in without seeming to.*
I told you not to annoy the gentleman with your rough tongue.

JOSIE
Sure I thought I was doing my duty as hostess making him feel at
home.

TYRONE
*Stares at her again.*
Why all the interest lately in the ladies of the profession, Josie?

JOSIE
Oh, I've been considering joining their union. It's easier living than
farming, I'm sure.
*Then resentfully.*
You think I'd starve at it, don't you, because your fancy is for dainty
dolls of women? But other men like—

TYRONE
*With sudden revulsion.*
For God's sake, cut out that kind of talk, Josie! It sounds like hell.

JOSIE
*Stares at him startledly—then resentfully.*
Oh, it does, does it?
*Forcing a scornful smile.*
I'm shocking you, I suppose?
HOGAN *is watching them both, not missing anything in their faces,
while he seems intent on his pipe.*

TYRONE
*Looking a bit sheepish and annoyed at himself for his interest—shrugs
his shoulders.*
No. Hardly. Forget it.
*He smiles kiddingly.*
Anyway, who told you I fall for the dainty dolls? That's all a thing
of the past. I like them tall and strong and voluptuous, now, with
beautiful big breasts.
*She blushes and looks confused and is furious with herself for doing so.*

38

HOGAN

There you are, Josie, darlin'. Sure he couldn't speak fairer than that.

JOSIE

*Recovers herself.*

He couldn't, indeed.

*She pats* TYRONE's *head—playfully.*

You're a terrible blarneying liar, Jim, but thank you just the same.

TYRONE *turns his attention to* HOGAN. *He winks at* JOSIE *and begins in an exaggeratedly casual manner.*

TYRONE

I don't blame you, Mr. Hogan, for taking it easy on such a blazing hot day.

HOGAN

*Doesn't look at him. His eyes twinkle.*

Hot, did you say? I find it cool, meself. Take off your coat if you're hot, Mister Tyrone.

TYRONE

One of the most stifling days I've ever known. Isn't it, Josie?

JOSIE

*Smiling.*

Terrible. I know you must be perishing.

HOGAN

I wouldn't call it a damned bit stifling.

TYRONE

It parches the membranes in your throat.

HOGAN

The what? Never mind. I can't have them, for my throat isn't parched at all. If yours is, Mister Tyrone, there's a well full of water at the back.

TYRONE

Water? That's something people wash with, isn't it? I mean, some people.

HOGAN

So I've heard. But, like you, I find it hard to believe. It's a dirty habit. They must be foreigners.

TYRONE

As I was saying, my throat is parched after the long dusty walk I took just for the pleasure of being your guest.

HOGAN

I don't remember inviting you, and the road is hard macadam with divil a spec of dust, and it's less than a quarter mile from the Inn here.

TYRONE

I didn't have a drink at the Inn. I was waiting until I arrived here, knowing that you—

HOGAN
Knowing I'd what?

TYRONE

Your reputation as a generous host—

HOGAN

The world must be full of liars. So you didn't have a drink at the Inn? Then it must be the air itself smells of whiskey today, although I didn't notice it before you came. You've gone on the water-wagon, I suppose? Well, that's fine, and I ask pardon for misjudging you.

TYRONE

I've wanted to go on the wagon for the past twenty-five years, but the doctors have strictly forbidden it. It would be fatal—with my weak heart.

HOGAN

So you've a weak heart? Well, well, and me thinking all along it was your head. I'm glad you told me. I was just going to offer you a drink, but whiskey is the worst thing—

TYRONE

The Docs say it's a matter of life and death. I must have a stimulant—one big drink, at least, whenever I strain my heart walking in the hot sun.

HOGAN
Walk back to the Inn, then, and give it a good strain, so you can buy yourself two big drinks.

JOSIE
*Laughing.*
Ain't you the fools, playing that old game between you, and both of you pleased as punch!

TYRONE
*Gives up with a laugh.*
Hasn't he ever been known to loosen up, Josie?

JOSIE
You ought to know. If you need a drink you'll have to buy it from him or die of thirst.

TYRONE
Well, I'll bet this is one time he's going to treat.

HOGAN
Be God, I'll take that bet!

TYRONE
After you've heard the news I've got for you, you'll be so delighted you won't be able to drag out the old bottle quick enough.

HOGAN
I'll have to be insanely delighted.

JOSIE
*Full of curiosity.*
Shut up, Father. What news, Jim?

TYRONE
I have it off the grapevine that a certain exalted personage will drop in on you before long.

HOGAN
It's the sheriff again. I know by the pleased look on your mug.

TYRONE
Not this time.
*He pauses tantalizingly.*

JOSIE
Bad luck to you, can't you tell us who?

TYRONE
A more eminent grafter than the sheriff—
*Sneeringly.*
A leading aristocrat in our Land of the Free and Get-Rich-Quick, whose boots are licked by one and all—one of the Kings of our Republic by Divine Right of Inherited Swag. In short, I refer to your good neighbor, T. Stedman Harder, Standard Oil's sappiest child, whom I know you both love so dearly.
*There is a pause after this announcement.* HOGAN *and* JOSIE *stiffen, and their eyes begin to glitter. But they can't believe their luck at first.*

HOGAN
*In an ominous whisper.*
Did you say Harder is coming to call on us, Jim?

JOSIE
It's too good to be true.

TYRONE
*Watching them with amusement.*
No kidding. The great Mr. Harder intends to stop here on his way back to lunch from a horseback ride.

JOSIE
How do you know?

TYRONE
Simpson told me. I ran into him at the Inn.

HOGAN
That English scum of a superintendent!

**TYRONE**

He was laughing himself sick. He said he suggested the idea to Harder—told him you'd be overwhelmed with awe if he deigned to interview you in person.

**HOGAN**

Overwhelmed isn't the word. Is it, Josie?

**JOSIE**

It isn't indeed, Father.

**TYRONE**

For once in his life, Simpson is cheering for you. He doesn't like his boss. In fact, he asked me to tell you he hopes you kill him.

**HOGAN**

*Disdainfully.*
To hell with the Limey's good wishes. I'd like both of them to call together.

**JOSIE**

Ah, well, we can't have everything.
*To* TYRONE.
What's the reason Mr. Harder decided to notice poor, humble scum the like of us?

**TYRONE**

*Grinning.*
That's right, Josie. Be humble. He'll expect you to know your place.

**HOGAN**

Will he now? Well, well.
*With a great happy sigh.*
This is going to be a beautiful day entirely.

**JOSIE**

But what's Harder's reason, Jim?

**TYRONE**

Well, it seems he has an ice pond on his estate.

HOGAN

Oho! So that's it!

TYRONE

Yes. That's it. Harder likes to keep up the good old manorial customs. He clings to his ice pond. And your pigpen isn't far from his ice pond.

HOGAN

A nice little stroll for the pigs, that's all.

TYRONE

And somehow Harder's fence in that vicinity has a habit of breaking down.

HOGAN

Fences are queer things. You can't depend on them.

TYRONE

Simpson says he's had it repaired a dozen times, but each time on the following night it gets broken down again.

JOSIE

What a strange thing! It must be the bad fairies. I can't imagine who else could have done it. Can you, Father?

HOGAN

I can't, surely.

TYRONE

Well, Simpson can. He knows you did it and he told his master so.

HOGAN

*Disdainfully.*

Master is the word. Sure, the English can't live unless they have a lord's backside to kiss, the dirty slaves.

TYRONE

The result of those breaks in the fence is that your pigs stroll—as you so gracefully put it—stroll through to wallow happily along the shores of the ice pond.

HOGAN

Well, why not? Sure, they're fine ambitious American-born pigs and they don't miss any opportunities. They're like Harder's father who made the money for him.

TYRONE

I agree, but for some strange reason Harder doesn't look forward to the taste of pig in next summer's ice water.

HOGAN

He must be delicate. Remember he's delicate, Josie, and leave your club in the house.
*He bursts into joyful menacing laughter.*
Oh, be God and be Christ in the mountains! I've pined to have a quiet word with Mr. Harder for years, watching him ride past in his big shiny automobile with his snoot in the air, and being tormented always by the complaints of his Limey superintendent. Oh, won't I welcome him!

JOSIE

Won't *we,* you mean. Sure, I love him as much as you.

HOGAN

I'd kiss you, Jim, for this beautiful news, if you wasn't so damned ugly. Maybe Josie'll do it for me. She has a stronger stomach.

JOSIE

I will! He's earned it.
*She pulls* TYRONE's *head back and laughingly kisses him on the lips. Her expression changes. She looks startled and confused, stirred and at the same time frightened. She forces a scornful laugh.*
Och, there's no spirit in you! It's like kissing a corpse.

TYRONE

*Gives her a strange surprised look—mockingly.*
Yes?
*Turning to* HOGAN.
Well, how about that drink, Phil? I'll leave it to Josie if drinks aren't on the house.

HOGAN

*I* won't leave it to Josie. She's prejudiced, being in love.

JOSIE

*Angrily.*

Shut up, you old liar!

*Then guiltily, forcing a laugh.*

Don't talk nonsense to sneak out of treating Jim.

HOGAN

*Sighing.*

All right, Josie. Go get the bottle and one small glass, or he'll never stop nagging me. I can turn my back, so the sight of him drinking free won't break my heart.

JOSIE *gets up, laughing, and goes in the house.* HOGAN *peers at the road off left.*

On his way back to lunch, you said? Then it's time—

*Fervently.*

O Holy Joseph, don't let the bastard change his mind!

TYRONE

*Beginning to have qualms.*

Listen, Phil. Don't get too enthusiastic. He has a big drag around here, and he'll have you pinched, sure as hell, if you beat him up.

HOGAN

Och, I'm no fool.

JOSIE *comes out with a bottle and a tumbler.*

Will you listen to this, Josie. He's warning me not to give Harder a beating—as if I'd dirty my hands on the scum.

JOSIE

As if we'd need to. Sure, all we want is a quiet chat with him.

HOGAN

That's all. As neighbor to neighbor.

JOSIE

*Hands* TYRONE *the bottle and tumbler.*

Here you are, Jim. Don't stint yourself.

46

HOGAN
*Mournfully.*
A fine daughter! I tell you a small glass and you give him a bucket!
*As* TYRONE *pours a big drink, grinning at him, he turns away with a comic shudder.*
That's a fifty-dollar drink, at least.

TYRONE
Here's luck, Phil.

HOGAN
I hope you drown.
TYRONE *drinks and makes a wry face.*

TYRONE
The best chicken medicine I've ever tasted.

HOGAN
That's gratitude for you! Here, pass me the bottle. A drink will warm up my welcome for His Majesty.
*He takes an enormous swig from the bottle.*

JOSIE
*Looking off left.*
There's two horseback riders on the county road now.

HOGAN
Praise be to God! It's him and a groom.
*He sets the bottle on top of the boulder.*

JOSIE
That's McCabe. An old sweetheart of mine.
*She glances at* TYRONE *provokingly—then suddenly worried and protective.*
You get in the house, Jim. If Harder sees you here, he'll lay the whole blame on you.

TYRONE
Nix, Josie. You don't think I'm going to miss this, do you?

JOSIE

You can sit inside by my window and take in everything. Come on, now, don't be stubborn with me.

*She puts her hands under his arms and lifts him to his feet as easily as if he was a child—banteringly.*

Go into my beautiful bedroom. It's a nice place for you.

TYRONE

*Kiddingly.*

Just what I've been thinking for some time, Josie.

JOSIE

*Boldly.*

Sure, you've never given me a sign of it. Come up tonight and we'll spoon in the moonlight and you can tell me your thoughts.

TYRONE

That's a date. Remember, now.

JOSIE

It's you who'll forget. Get inside now, before it's too late.

*She gives him a shove inside and closes the door.*

HOGAN

*Has been watching the visitor approach.*

He's dismounting—as graceful as a scarecrow, and his poor horse longing to give him a kick. Look at Mac grinning at us. Sit down, Josie.

*She sits on the steps, he on the boulder.*

Pretend you don't notice him.

T. STEDMAN HARDER *appears at left. They act as if they didn't see him.* HOGAN *knocks out his pipe on the palm of his hand.*

HARDER *is in his late thirties but looks younger because his face is unmarked by worry, ambition, or any of the common hazards of life. No matter how long he lives, his four undergraduate years will always be for him the most significant in his life, and the moment of his highest achievement the time he was tapped for an exclusive Senior Society at the Ivy university to which his father had given millions. Since that day*

48

*he has felt no need for further aspiring, no urge to do anything except settle down on his estate and live the life of a country gentleman, mildly interested in saddle horses and sport models of foreign automobiles. He is not the blatantly silly, playboy heir to millions whose antics make newspaper headlines. He doesn't drink much except when he attends his class reunion every spring—the most exciting episode of each year for him. He doesn't give wild parties, doesn't chase after musical-comedy cuties, is a mildly contented husband and father of three children. A not unpleasant man, affable, good-looking in an ordinary way, sunburnt and healthy, beginning to take on fat, he is simply immature, naturally lethargic, a bit stupid. Coddled from birth, everything arranged and made easy for him, deferred to because of his wealth, he usually has the self-confident attitude of acknowledged superiority, but assumes a supercilious, insecure air when dealing with people beyond his ken. He is dressed in a beautifully tailored English tweed coat and whipcord riding breeches, immaculately polished English riding boots with spurs, and carries a riding crop in his hand.*

*It would be hard to find anyone more ill-equipped for combat with the* HOGANS. *He has never come in contact with anyone like them. To make matters easier for them he is deliberate in his speech, slow on the uptake, and has no sense of humor. The experienced strategy of the* HOGANS *in verbal battle is to take the offensive at once and never let an opponent get set to hit back. Also, they use a beautifully co-ordinated, bewildering change of pace, switching suddenly from jarring shouts to low, confidential vituperation. And they exaggerate their Irish brogues to confuse an enemy still further.*

HARDER
*Walks toward* HOGAN—*stiffly.*
Good morning. I want to see the man who runs this farm.

HOGAN
*Surveys him deliberately, his little pig eyes gleaming with malice.*
You do, do you? Well, you've seen him. So run along now and play with your horse, and don't bother me.
*He turns to* JOSIE, *who is staring at* HARDER, *much to his discomfiture, as if she had discovered a cockroach in her soup.*

49

D'you see what I see, Josie? Be God, you'll have to give that damned cat of yours a spanking for bringing it to our doorstep.

HARDER
*Determined to be authoritative and command respect — curtly.*
Are you Hogan?

HOGAN
*Insultingly.*
I am *Mister* Philip Hogan — to a gentleman.

JOSIE
*Glares at* HARDER.
Where's your manners, you spindle-shanked jockey? Were you brought up in a stable?

HARDER
*Does not fight with ladies, and especially not with this lady — ignoring her.*
My name is Harder.
*He obviously expects them to be immediately impressed and apologetic.*

HOGAN
*Contemptuously.*
Who asked you your name, me little man?

JOSIE
Sure, who in the world cares who the hell you are?

HOGAN
But if you want to play politeness, we'll play with you. Let me introduce you to my daughter, Harder — Miss Josephine Hogan.

JOSIE
*Petulantly.*
I don't want to meet him, Father. I don't like his silly sheep's face, and I've no use for jockeys, anyway. I'll wager he's no damned good to a woman.
*From inside her bedroom comes a burst of laughter. This revelation of an unseen audience startles* HARDER. *He begins to look extremely unsure of himself.*

50

HOGAN

I don't think he's a jockey. It's only the funny pants he's wearing. I'll
bet if you asked his horse, you'd find he's no cowboy either.
*To* HARDER, *jeeringly.*
Come, tell us the truth, me honey. Don't you kiss your horse each
time you mount and beg him, please don't throw me today, darlin',
and I'll give you an extra bucket of oats.
*He bursts into an extravagant roar of laughter, slapping his thigh, and*
JOSIE *guffaws with him, while they watch the disconcerting effect of this
theatrical mirth on* HARDER.

HARDER

*Beginning to lose his temper.*
Listen to me, Hogan! I didn't come here—
*He is going to add "to listen to your damned jokes" or something like that,
but* HOGAN *silences him.*

HOGAN

*Shouts.*
What? What's that you said?
*He stares at the dumbfounded* HARDER *with droll amazement, as if he
couldn't believe his ears.*
You didn't come here?
*He turns to* JOSIE—*in a whisper.*
Did you hear that, Josie?
*He takes off his hat and scratches his head in comic bewilderment.*
Well, that's a puzzle, surely. How d'you suppose he got here?

JOSIE

Maybe the stork brought him, bad luck to it for a dirty bird.
*Again* TYRONE'S *laughter is heard from the bedroom.*

HARDER

*So off balance now he can only repeat angrily.*
I said I didn't come here—

HOGAN

*Shouts.*
Wait! Wait, now!

*Threateningly.*

We've had enough of that. Say it a third time and I'll send my daughter to telephone the asylum.

HARDER
*Forgetting he's a gentleman.*
Damn you, I'm the one who's had enough—!

JOSIE
*Shouts.*
Hold your dirty tongue! I'll have no foul language in my presence.

HOGAN
Och, don't mind him, Josie. He's said he isn't here, anyway, so we won't talk to him behind his back.
*He regards* HARDER *with pitying contempt.*
Sure, ain't you the poor crazy creature? Do you want us to believe you're your own ghost?

HARDER
*Notices the bottle on the boulder for the first time—tries to be contemptuously tolerant and even to smile with condescending disdain.*
Ah! I understand now. You're drunk. I'll come back sometime when you're sober—or send Simpson—
*He turns away, glad of an excuse to escape.*

JOSIE
*Jumps up and advances on him menacingly.*
No, you don't! You'll apologize first for insulting a lady—insinuating I'm drunk this early in the day—or I'll knock some good breeding in you!

HARDER
*Actually frightened now.*
I—I said nothing about you—

HOGAN
*Gets up to come between them.*
Aisy now, Josie. He didn't mean it. He don't know what he means, the poor loon.

*To* HARDER—*pityingly.*
Run home, that's a good lad, before your keeper misses you.

HARDER
*Hastily.*
Good day.
*He turns eagerly toward left but suddenly* HOGAN *grabs his shoulder
and spins him around—then shifts his grip to the lapel of* HARDER'S
*coat.*

HOGAN
*Grimly.*
Wait now, me Honey Boy. I'll have a word with you, if you plaze. I'm
beginning to read some sense into this. You mentioned that English
bastard, Simpson. I know who you are now.

HARDER
*Outraged.*
Take your hands off me, you drunken fool.
*He raises his riding crop.*

JOSIE
*Grabs it and tears it from his hand with one powerful twist—fiercely.*
Would you strike my poor infirm old father, you coward, you!

HARDER
*Calling for help.*
McCabe!

HOGAN
Don't think McCabe will hear you, if you blew Gabriel's horn. He
knows I or Josie can lick him with one hand.
*Sharply.*
Josie! Stand between us and the gate.
JOSIE *takes her stand where the path meets the road. She turns her back
for a moment, shaking with suppressed laughter, and waves her hand at*
MC CABE *and turns back.* HOGAN *releases his hold on* HARDER'S *coat.*
There now. Don't try running away or my daughter will knock you
senseless.
*He goes on grimly before* HARDER *can speak.*

53

You're the blackguard of a millionaire that owns the estate next to ours, ain't you? I've been meaning to call on you, for I've a bone to pick with you, you bloody tyrant! But I couldn't bring myself to set foot on land bought with Standard Oil money that was stolen from the poor it ground in the dust beneath its dirty heel—land that's watered with the tears of starving widows and orphans—

*He abruptly switches from this eloquence to a matter-of-fact tone.*

But never mind that, now. I won't waste words trying to reform a born crook.

*Fiercely, shoving his dirty unshaven face almost into* HARDER'S.

What I want to know is, what the hell d'you mean by your contemptible trick of breaking down your fence to entice my poor pigs to take their death in your ice pond?

*There is a shout of laughter from* JOSIE's *bedroom, and* JOSIE *doubles up and holds her sides.* HARDER *is so flabbergasted by this mad accusation he cannot even sputter. But* HOGAN *acts as if he'd denied it—savagely.*

Don't lie, now! None of your damned Standard Oil excuses, or be Jaysus, I'll break you in half! Haven't I mended that fence morning after morning, and seen the footprints where you had sneaked up in the night to pull it down again. How many times have I mended that fence, Josie?

JOSIE

If it's once, it's a hundred, Father.

HOGAN

Listen, me little millionaire! I'm a peaceful, mild man that believes in live and let live, and as long as the neighboring scum leave me alone, I'll let them alone, but when it comes to standing by and seeing my poor pigs murthered one by one—! Josie! How many pigs is it caught their death of cold in his damned ice pond and died of pneumonia?

JOSIE

Ten of them, Father. And ten more died of cholera after drinking the dirty water in it.

HOGAN

All prize pigs, too! I was offered two hundred dollars apiece for them.
Twenty pigs at two hundred, that's four thousand. And a thousand
to cure the sick and cover funeral expenses for the dead. Call it four
thousand you owe me.

*Furiously.*

And you'll pay it, or I'll sue you, so help me Christ! I'll drag you in
every court in the land! I'll paste your ugly mug on the front page
of every newspaper as a pig-murdering tyrant! Before I'm through
with you, you'll think you're the King of England at an Irish wake!

*With a quick change of pace to a wheedling confidential tone.*

Tell me now, if it isn't a secret, whatever made you take such a sav-
age grudge against pigs? Sure, it isn't reasonable for a Standard Oil
man to hate hogs.

HARDER

*Manages to get in three sputtering words.*

I've had enough—!

HOGAN

*With a grin.*

Be God, I believe you!

*Switching to fierceness and grabbing his lapel again.*

Look out, now! Keep your place and be soft-spoken to your bet-
ters! You're not in your shiny automobile now with your funny nose
cocked so you won't smell the poor people.

*He gives him a shake.*

And let me warn you! I have to put up with a lot of pests on this heap
of boulders some joker once called a farm. There's a cruel skinflint
of a landlord who swindles me out of my last drop of whiskey, and
there's poison ivy, and ticks and potato bugs, and there's snakes and
skunks! But, be God, I draw the line somewhere, and I'll be damned
if I'll stand for a Standard Oil man trespassing! So will you kindly
get the hell out of here before I plant a kick on your backside that'll
land you in the Atlantic Ocean!

*He gives* HARDER *a shove.*

Beat it now!

HARDER *tries to make some sort of disdainfully dignified exit. But he has to get by* JOSIE.

JOSIE
*Leers at him idiotically.*
Sure, you wouldn't go without a word of good-bye to me, would you, darlin'? Don't scorn me just because you have on your jockey's pants.
*In a hoarse whisper.*
Meet me tonight, as usual, down by the pigpen.
HARDER'*s retreat becomes a rout. He disappears on left, but a second later his voice, trembling with anger, is heard calling back threateningly.*

HARDER
If you dare touch that fence again, I'll put this matter in the hands of the police!

HOGAN
*Shouts derisively.*
And I'll put it in my lawyer's hands and in the newspapers!
*He doubles up with glee.*
Look at him fling himself on his nag and spur the poor beast! And look at McCabe behind him! He can hardly stay in the saddle for laughing!
*He slaps his thigh.*
O Jaysus, this is a great day for the poor and oppressed! I'll do no more work! I'll go down to the Inn and spend money and get drunk as Moses!

JOSIE
Small blame to you. You deserve it. But you'll have your dinner first, to give you a foundation. Come on, now.
*They turn back toward the house. From inside another burst of laughter from* TYRONE *is heard.* JOSIE *smiles.*
Listen to Jim still in stitches. It's good to hear him laugh as if he meant it.
TYRONE *appears in the doorway of her bedroom.*

TYRONE
O God, my sides are sore.

56

*They all laugh together. He joins them at the left corner of the house.*

JOSIE

It's dinner time. Will you have a bite to eat with us, Jim? I'll boil you some eggs.

HOGAN

Och, why do you have to mention eggs? Don't you know it's the one thing he might eat? Well, no matter. Anything goes today.
*He gets the bottle of whiskey.*
Come in, Jim. We'll have a drink while Josie's fixing the grub.
*They start to go in the front door,* HOGAN *in the lead.*

TYRONE

*Suddenly—with sardonic amusement.*
Wait a minute. Let us pause to take a look at this very valuable property. Don't you notice the change, Phil? Every boulder on the place has turned to solid gold.

HOGAN

What the hell—? You didn't get the D.T.'s from my whiskey, I know that.

TYRONE

No D.T.'s about it. This farm has suddenly become a gold mine. You know that offer I told you about? Well, the agent did a little detective work and he discovered it came from Harder. He doesn't want the damned place but he dislikes you as a neighbor and he thinks the best way to get rid of you would be to become your landlord.

HOGAN

The sneaking skunk! I'm sorry I didn't give him that kick.

TYRONE

Yes. So am I. That would have made the place even more valuable. But as it is, you did nobly. I expect him to double or triple his first offer. In fact, I'll bet the sky is the limit now.

HOGAN

*Gives* JOSIE *a meaningful look.*

I see your point! But we're not worrying you'd ever forget your promise to us for any price.

TYRONE

Promise? What promise? You know what Kipling wrote.
*Paraphrasing the "Rhyme of the Three Sealers."*
There's never a promise of God or man goes north of ten thousand bucks.

HOGAN

D'you hear him, Josie? We can't trust him.

JOSIE

Och, you know he's kidding.

HOGAN

I don't! I'm becoming suspicious.

TYRONE

*A trace of bitterness beneath his amused tone.*
That's wise dope, Phil. Trust and be a sucker. If I were you, I'd be seriously worried. I've always wanted to own a gold mine—so I could sell it.

JOSIE

*Bursts out.*
Will you shut up your rotten Broadway blather!

TYRONE

*Stares at her in surprise.*
Why so serious and indignant, Josie? You just told your unworthy Old Man I was kidding.
*To* HOGAN.
At last, I've got you by the ears, Phil. We must have a serious chat about when you're going to pay that back rent.

HOGAN

*Groans.*
A landlord who's a blackmailer! Holy God, what next!
JOSIE *is smiling with relief now.*

TYRONE

And you, Josie, please remember when I keep that moonlight date tonight I expect you to be very sweet to me.

JOSIE

*With a bold air.*

Sure, you don't have to blackmail me. I'd be that to you, anyway.

HOGAN

Are you laying plots in my presence to seduce my only daughter?

*Then philosophically.*

Well, what can I do? I'll be drunk at the Inn, so how could I prevent it?

*He goes up the steps.*

Let's eat, for the love of God. I'm starving.

*He disappears inside the house.*

JOSIE

*With an awkward playful gesture, takes* TYRONE *by the hand.*

Come along, Jim.

TYRONE

*Smiles kiddingly.*

Afraid you'll lose me? Swell chance!

*His eyes fix on her breasts—with genuine feeling.*

You have the most beautiful breasts in the world, do you know it, Josie?

JOSIE

*Pleased—shyly.*

I don't—but I'm happy if you think—

*Then quickly.*

But I've no time now to listen to your kidding, with my mad old father waiting for his dinner. So come on.

*She tugs at his hand and he follows her up the steps. Her manner changes to worried solicitude.*

Promise me you'll eat something, Jim. You've got to eat. You can't go on the way you are, drinking and never eating, hardly. You're killing yourself.

**TYRONE**
*Sardonically.*
That's right. Mother me, Josie, I love it.

**JOSIE**
*Bullyingly.*
I will, then. You need one to take care of you.
*They disappear inside the house.*

CURTAIN

# Act Two

*The same, with the wall of the living room removed. It is a clear warm moonlight night, around eleven o'clock.*

JOSIE *is sitting on the steps before the front door. She has changed to her Sunday best, a cheap dark-blue dress, black stockings and shoes. Her hair is carefully arranged, and by way of adornment a white flower is pinned on her bosom. She is hunched up, elbows on knees, her chin in her hands. There is an expression on her face we have not seen before, a look of sadness and loneliness and humiliation.*

*She sighs and gets slowly to her feet, her body stiff from sitting long in the same position. She goes into the living room, fumbles around for a box of matches, and lights a kerosene lamp on the table.*

*The living room is small, low-ceilinged, with faded, fly-specked wallpaper, a floor of bare boards. It is cluttered up with furniture that looks as if it had been picked up at a fire sale. There is a table at center, a disreputable old Morris chair beside it; two ugly sideboards, one at left, the other at right-rear; a porch rocking-chair, painted green, with a hole in its cane bottom; a bureau against the rear wall, with two chairs on either side of a door to the kitchen. On the bureau is an alarm clock which shows the time to be five past eleven. At right-front is the door to* JOSIE'S *bedroom.*

JOSIE
*Looks at the clock—dully.*
Five past eleven, and he said he'd be here around nine.

*Suddenly in a burst of humiliated anger, she tears off the flower pinned to her bosom and throws it in the corner.*

To hell with you, Jim Tyrone!

*From down the road, the quiet of the night is shattered by a burst of melancholy song. It is unmistakably* HOGAN'*s voice wailing an old Irish lament at the top of his lungs.* JOSIE *starts—then frowns irritably.*

What's bringing him home an hour before the Inn closes? He must be more paralyzed than ever I've known him.

*She listens to the singing—grimly.*

Ah, here you come, do you, full as a tick! I'll give you a welcome, if you start cutting up! I'm in no mood to put up with you.

*She goes into her bedroom and returns with her broomstick club. Outside the singing grows louder as* HOGAN *approaches the house. He only remembers one verse of the song and he has been repeating it.*

HOGAN

> *Oh the praties they grow small*
> *Over here, over here,*
> *Oh, the praties they grow small*
> *Over here.*
> *Oh the praties they grow small*
> *And we dig them in the fall*
> *And we eat them skins and all*
> *Over here, over here.*

*He enters left-front, weaving and lurching a bit. But he is not as drunk as he appears. Or rather, he is one of those people who can drink an enormous amount and be absolutely plastered when they want to be for their own pleasure, but at the same time are able to pull themselves together when they wish and be cunningly clear-headed. Just now, he is letting himself go and getting great satisfaction from it. He pauses and bellows belligerently at the house.*

Hurroo! Down with all tyrants, male and female! To hell with England, and God damn Standard Oil!

JOSIE

*Shouts back.*

Shut up your noise, you crazy old billy goat!

HOGAN

*Hurt and mournful.*

A sweet daughter and a sweet welcome home in the dead of night.

*Beginning to boil.*

Old goat! There's respect for you!

*Angrily—starting for the front door.*

Crazy billy goat, is it? Be God, I'll learn you manners!

*He pounds on the door with his fist.*

Open the door! Open this door, I'm saying, before I drive a fist through it, or kick it into flinders!

*He gives it a kick.*

JOSIE

It's not locked, you drunken old loon! Open it yourself!

HOGAN

*Turns the knob and stamps in.*

Drunken old loon, am I? Is that the way to address your father?

JOSIE

No. It's too damned good for him.

HOGAN

It's time I taught you a lesson. Be Jaysus, I'll take you over my knee and spank your tail, if you are as big as a cow!

*He makes a lunge to grab her.*

JOSIE

Would you, though! Take that, then!

*She raps him smartly, but lightly, on his bald spot with the end of her broom handle.*

HOGAN

*With an exaggerated howl of pain.*

Ow!

*His anger evaporates and he rubs the top of his head ruefully—with bitter complaint.*

God forgive you, it's a great shame to me I've raised a daughter so cowardly she has to use a club.

JOSIE

*Puts her club on the table—grimly.*

Now I've no club.

HOGAN

*Evades the challenge.*

I never thought I'd see the day when a daughter of mine would be such a coward as to threaten her old father when he's helpless drunk and can't hit back.

*He slumps down on the Morris chair.*

JOSIE

Ah, that's better. Now that little game is over.

*Then angrily.*

Listen to me, Father. I have no patience left, so get up from that chair, and go in your room, and go to bed, or I'll take you by the scruff of your neck and the seat of your pants and throw you in and lock the door on you! I mean it, now!

*On the verge of angry tears.*

I've had all I can bear this night, and I want some peace and sleep, and not to listen to an old lush!

HOGAN

*Appears drunker, his head wagging, his voice thick, his talk rambling.*

That's right. Fight with me. My own daughter has no feelings or sympathy. As if I hadn't enough after what's happened tonight.

JOSIE

*With angry disgust.*

Och, don't try—

*Then curiously.*

What's happened? I thought something must be queer, you coming home before the Inn closed, but then I thought maybe for once you'd drunk all you could hold.

*Scathingly.*

And, God pity you, if you ain't that full, you're damned close to it.

HOGAN

Go on. Make fun of me. Old lush! You wouldn't feel so comical, if—

*He stops, mumbling to himself.*

JOSIE
If what?

HOGAN
Never mind. Never mind. I didn't come home to fight, but seek comfort in your company. And if I was singing coming along the road, it was only because there's times you have to sing to keep from crying.

JOSIE
I can see you crying!

HOGAN
You will. And you'll see yourself crying, too, when—
*He stops again and mumbles to himself.*

JOSIE
When what?
*Exasperatedly.*
Will you stop your whiskey drooling and talk plain?

HOGAN
*Thickly.*
No matter. No matter. Leave me alone.

JOSIE
*Angrily.*
That's good advice. To hell with you! I know your game. Nothing at all has happened. All you want is to keep me up listening to your guff. Go to your room, I'm saying, before—

HOGAN
I won't. I couldn't sleep with my thoughts tormented the way they are. I'll stay here in this chair, and you go to your room and let me be.

JOSIE
*Snorts.*
And have you singing again in a minute and smashing the furniture—

HOGAN

Sing, is it? Are you making fun again? I'd give a keen of sorrow or howl at the moon like an old mangy hound in his sadness if I knew how, but I don't. So rest aisy. You won't hear a sound from me. Go on and snore like a pig to your heart's content.

*He mourns drunkenly.*

A fine daughter! I'd get more comfort from strangers.

JOSIE

Och, for God's sake, dry up! You'll sit in the dark then. I won't leave the lamp lit for you to tip over and burn down the house.

*She reaches out to turn down the lamp.*

HOGAN

*Thickly.*

Let it burn to the ground. A hell of a lot I care if it burns.

JOSIE

*In the act of turning down the lamp, stops and stares at him, puzzled and uneasy.*

I never heard you talk that way before, no matter how drunk you were.

*He mumbles. Her tone becomes persuasive.*

What's happened to you, Father?

HOGAN

*Bitterly.*

Ah it's "Father" now, is it, not old billy goat? Well, thank God for small favors.

*With heavy sarcasm.*

Oh, nothing's happened to me at all, at all. A trifle, only. I wouldn't waste your time mentioning it, or keep you up when you want sleep so bad.

JOSIE

*Angrily.*

Och, you old loon, I'm sick of you. Sleep it off till you get some sense.

*She reaches for the lamp again.*

HOGAN

Sleep it off? We'll see if you'll sleep it off when you know—
*He lapses into drunken mumbling.*

JOSIE

*Again stares at him.*
Know what, Father?

HOGAN

*Mumbles.*
The son of a bitch!

JOSIE

*Trying a light tone.*
Sure, there's a lot of those in the neighborhood. Which one do you mean? Is Harder on your mind again?

HOGAN

*Thickly.*
He's one and a prize one, but I don't mean him. I'll say this for Harder, you know what to expect from him. He's no wolf in sheep's clothing, nor a treacherous snake in the grass who stabs you in the back with a knife—

JOSIE

*Apprehensive now—forces a joke.*
Sure, if you've found a snake who can stab you with a knife, you'd better join the circus with him and make a pile of money.

HOGAN

*Bitterly.*
Make jokes, God forgive you! You'll soon laugh from the wrong end of your mouth!
*He mumbles.*
Pretending he's our friend! The lying bastard!

JOSIE

*Bristles resentfully.*
Is it Jim Tyrone you're calling hard names?

HOGAN

That's right. Defend him, you big soft fool! Faith, you're a prize
dunce! You've had a good taste of believing his word, waiting hours
for him dressed up in your best like a poor sheep without pride or
spirit—

JOSIE

*Stung.*

Shut up! I was calling him a lying bastard myself before you came,
and saying I'd never speak to him again. And I knew all along he'd
never remember to keep his date after he got drunk.

HOGAN

He's not so drunk he forgot to attend to business.

JOSIE

*As if she hadn't heard—defiantly.*

I'd have stayed up anyway a beautiful night like this to enjoy the
moonlight, if there wasn't a Jim Tyrone in the world.

HOGAN

*With heavy sarcasm.*

In your best shoes and stockings? Well, well. Sure, the moon must
feel flattered by your attentions.

JOSIE

*Furiously.*

You won't feel flattered if I knock you tail over tin cup out of that
chair! And stop your whiskey gabble about Jim. I see what you're
driving at with your dark hints and curses, and if you think I'll believe—

*With forced assurance.*

Sure, I know what's happened as well as if I'd been there. Jim saw
you'd got drunker than usual and you were an easy mark for a joke,
and he's made a goat of you!

HOGAN

*Bitterly.*

Goat, again!

68

*He struggles from his chair and stands swaying unsteadily—with offended dignity.*
All right, I won't say another word. There's no use telling the truth to a bad-tempered woman in love.

JOSIE

Love be damned! I hate him now!

HOGAN

Be Christ, you have me stumped. A great proud slut who's played games with half the men around here, and now you act like a numbskull virgin that can't believe a man would tell her a lie!

JOSIE

*Threateningly.*
If you're going to your room, you'd better go quick!

HOGAN

*Fixes his eyes on the door at rear—with dignity.*
That's where I'm going, yes—to talk to meself so I'll know someone with brains is listening. Good night to you, Miss Hogan.
*He starts—swerves left—tries to correct this and lurches right and bumps against her, clutching the supporting arm she stretches out.*

JOSIE

God help you, if you try to go upstairs now, you'll end up in the cellar.

HOGAN

*Hanging on to her arm and shoulder—maudlinly affectionate now.*
You're right. Don't listen to me. I'm wrong to bother you. You've had sorrow enough this night. Have a good sleep, while you can, Josie, darlin'—and good night and God bless you.
*He tries to kiss her, but she wards him off and steers him back to the chair.*

JOSIE

Sit down before you split in pieces on the floor and I have to get the wheelbarrow to collect you.

*She dumps him in the chair where he sprawls limply, his chin on his chest.*

HOGAN
*Mumbles dully.*
It's too late. It's all settled. We're helpless, entirely.

JOSIE
*Really worried now.*
How is it all settled? If you're helpless, I'm not.
*Then as he doesn't reply—scornfully.*
It's the first time I ever heard you admit you were licked. And it's the first time I ever saw you so paralyzed you couldn't shake the whiskey from your brains and get your head clear when you wanted. Sure, that's always been your pride—and now look at you, the stupid object you are, mumbling and drooling!

HOGAN
*Struggles up in his chair—angrily.*
Shut up your insults! Be God, I can get my head clear if I like!
*He shakes his head violently.*
There! It's clear. I can tell you each thing that happened tonight as clear as if I'd not taken a drop, if you'll listen and not keep calling me a liar.

JOSIE
I'll listen, now I see you have hold of your wits.

HOGAN
All right, then. I'll begin at the beginning when him and me left here, and you gave him a sweet smile, and rolled your big beautiful cow's eyes at him, and wiggled your backside, and stuck out your beautiful breasts you know he admires, and said in a sick sheep's voice: "Don't forget our moonlight date, Jim."

JOSIE
*With suppressed fury.*
You're a—! I never—! You old—!

HOGAN

And he said: "You bet I won't forget, Josie."

JOSIE

The lying crook!

HOGAN

*His voice begins to sink into a dejected monotone.*
We went to the Inn and started drinking whiskey. And I got drunk.

JOSIE

*Exasperatedly.*
I guessed that! And Jim got drunk, too. And then what?

HOGAN

*Dully.*
Who knows how drunk he got? He had one of his queer fits when
you can't tell. He's the way I told you about this morning, when
he talks like a Broadway crook, who'd sell his soul for a price, and
there's a sneering divil in him, and he loves to pick out the weakness
in people and say cruel, funny things that flay the hide off them, or
play cruel jokes on them.
*With sudden rage.*
God's curse on him, I'll wager he's laughing to himself this minute,
thinking it's the cutest joke in the world, the fools he's made of us.
You in particular. Be God, I had my suspicions, at least, but your
head was stuffed with mush and love, and you wouldn't—

JOSIE

*Furiously.*
You'll tell that lie about my love once too often! And I'll play a joke
on him yet that'll make him sorry he—

HOGAN

*Sunk in drunken defeatism again.*
It's too late. You shouldn't have let him get away from you to the
Inn. You should have kept him here. Then maybe, if you'd got him
drunk enough you could have—
*His head nodding, his eyes blinking—thickly.*
But it's no good talking now—no good at all—no good—

71

JOSIE
*Gives him a shake.*
Keep hold of your wits or I'll give you a cuff on both ears! Will
you stop blathering like an old woman and tell me plainly what he's
done!

HOGAN
He's agreed to sell the farm, that's what! Simpson came to the Inn
to see him with a new offer from Harder. Ten thousand, cash.

JOSIE
*Overwhelmed.*
Ten thousand! Sure, three is all it's worth at most. And two was what
you offered that Jim promised—

HOGAN
What's money to Harder? After what we did to him, all he wants is
revenge. And here's where he's foxy. Simpson must have put him up
to it knowing how Jim hates it here living on a small allowance, and
he longs to go back to Broadway and his whores. Jim won't have to
wait for his half of the cash till the estate's settled. Harder offers to
give him five thousand cash as a loan against the estate the second
the sale is made. Jim can take the next train to New York.

JOSIE
*Tensely, on the verge of tears.*
And Jim accepted? I don't believe it!

HOGAN
Don't then. Be God, you'll believe it tomorrow! Harder proposed
that he meet with Jim and the executors in the morning and settle
it, and Jim promised Simpson he would.

JOSIE
*Desperately.*
Maybe he'll get so drunk he'll never remember—

HOGAN
He won't. Harder's coming in his automobile to pick him up and
make sure of him. Anyway don't think because he forgot you were

waiting—in the moonlight, eating your heart out, that he'd ever miss a date with five thousand dollars, and all the pretty whores of Broadway he can buy with it.

JOSIE

*Distractedly.*

Will you shut up!

*Angrily.*

And where were you when all this happened? Couldn't you do anything to stop it, you old loon?

HOGAN

I couldn't. Simpson came and sat at the table with us—

JOSIE

And you let him!

HOGAN

Jim invited him. Anyway, I wanted to find out what trick he had up his sleeve, and what Jim would do. When it was all over, I got up and took a swipe at Simpson, but I missed him.

*With drunken sadness.*

I was too drunk—too drunk—too drunk—I missed him, God forgive me!

*His chin sinks on his chest and his eyes shut.*

JOSIE

*Shakes him.*

If you don't keep awake, be God, I won't miss you!

HOGAN

I was going to take a swipe at Jim, too, but I couldn't do it. My heart was too broken with sorrow. I'd come to love him like a son—a real son of my heart!—to take the place of that jackass, Mike, and me two other jackasses.

JOSIE

*Her face hard and bitter.*

I think now Mike was the only one in this house with sense.

HOGAN

I was too drowned in sorrow by his betraying me—and you he'd pretended to like so much. So I only called him a dirty lying skunk of a treacherous bastard, and I turned my back on him and left the Inn, and I made myself sing on the road so he'd hear, and they'd all hear in the Inn, to show them I didn't care a damn.

JOSIE

*Scathingly.*

Sure, wasn't you the hero! A hell of a lot of good—

HOGAN

Ah, well, I suppose the temptation was too great. He's weak, with one foot in the grave from whiskey. Maybe we shouldn't blame him.

JOSIE

*Her eyes flashing.*

Not blame him? Well, I blame him, God damn him! Are you making excuses for him, you old fool!

HOGAN

I'm not. He's a dirty snake! But I was thinking how do I know what I wouldn't do for five thousand cash, and how do you know what you wouldn't do?

JOSIE

Nothing could make me betray him!

*Her face grows hard and bitter.*

Or it couldn't before. There's nothing I wouldn't do now.

HOGAN *suddenly begins to chuckle.*

Do you think I'm lying? Just give me a chance—

HOGAN

I remembered something.

*He laughs drunkenly.*

Be Christ, Josie, for all his Broadway wisdom about women, you've made a prize damned fool of him and that's some satisfaction!

JOSIE
*Bewildered.*
How'd you mean?

HOGAN
You'll never believe it. Neither did I, but he kept on until, be God, I saw he really meant it.

JOSIE
Meant what?

HOGAN
It was after he'd turned queer—early in the night before Simpson came. He started talking about you, as if you was on his mind, worrying him—and before he finished I take my oath I began to hope you could really work Mike's first scheme on him, if you got him alone in the moonlight, because all his gab was about his great admiration for you.

JOSIE
Och! The liar!

HOGAN
He said you had great beauty in you that no one appreciated but him.

JOSIE
*Shakenly.*
You're lying.

HOGAN
Great strength you had, and great pride, he said—and great goodness, no less! But here's where you've made a prize jackass of him, like I said.
*With a drunken leer.*
Listen now, darlin', and don't drop dead with amazement.
*He leans toward her and whispers.*
He believes you're a virgin!
JOSIE *stiffens as if she'd been insulted,* HOGAN *goes on.*
He does, so help me! He means it, the poor dunce! He thinks you're

75

a poor innocent virgin! He thinks it's all boasting and pretending you've done about being a slut.

*He chuckles.*

A virgin, no less! You!

JOSIE

*Furiously.*

Stop saying it! Boasting and pretending, am I? The dirty liar!

HOGAN

Faith, you don't have to tell me.

*Then he looks at her in drunken surprise—thickly.*

Are you taking it as an insult? Why the hell don't you laugh? Be God, you ought to see what a stupid sheep that makes him.

JOSIE

*Forces a laugh.*

I do see it.

HOGAN

*Chuckling drunkenly.*

Oh, be God, I've just remembered another thing, Josie. I know why he didn't keep his date with you. It wasn't that he'd forgot. He remembered well enough, for he talked about it—

JOSIE

You mean he deliberately, knowing I'd be waiting—

*Fiercely.*

God damn him!

HOGAN

He as much as told me his reason, though he wouldn't come out with it plain, me being your father. His conscience was tormenting him. He's going to leave you alone and not see you again—for your sake, because he loves you!

*He chuckles.*

JOSIE

*Looks stricken and bewildered—her voice trembling.*

Loves me? You're making it up.

HOGAN

I'm not. I know it sounds crazy but—

JOSIE

What did he mean, for my sake?

HOGAN

Can't you see? You're a pure virgin to him, but all the same there's things besides your beautiful soul he feels drawn to, like your beautiful hair and eyes, and—

JOSIE

*Strickenly.*
Och, don't, Father! You know I'm only a big—

HOGAN

*As if she hadn't spoken.*
So he'll keep away from temptation because he can't trust himself, and it'd be a sin on his conscience if he was to seduce you.
*He laughs drunkenly.*
Oh, be God! If that ain't rich!

JOSIE

*Her voice trembles.*
So that was his reason—
*Then angrily.*
So he thinks all he has to do is crook a finger and I'll fall for him, does he, the vain Broadway crook!

HOGAN

*Chuckling.*
Be Jaysus, it was the maddest thing in the world, him gabbing like a soft loon about you—and there at the bar in plain sight was two of the men you've been out with, the gardener at Smith's and Regan, the chauffeur for Driggs, having a drink together!

JOSIE

*With a twitching smile.*
It must have been mad, surely. I wish I'd been there to laugh up my sleeve.

*Angry.*
But what's all his crazy lying blather got to do with him betraying us and selling the place?

HOGAN
*At once hopelessly dejected again.*
Nothing at all. I only thought you'd like to know you'd had that much revenge.

JOSIE
A hell of a revenge! I'll have a better one than that on him— or I'll try to! I'm not like you, owning up I'm beaten and crying wurra-wurra like a coward and getting hopeless drunk!
*She gives him a shake.*
Get your wits about you and answer me this: Did Simpson get him to sign a paper?

HOGAN
No, but what good is that? In the morning he'll sign all they shove in front of him.

JOSIE
It's this good. It means we still have a chance. Or I have.

HOGAN
What chance? Are you going to beg him to take pity on us?

JOSIE
I'll see him in hell first! There's another chance, and a good one. But I'll need your help—
*Angrily.*
And look at you, your brains drowned in whiskey, so I can't depend on you!

HOGAN
*Rousing himself.*
You can, if there's any chance. Be God, I'll make myself as sober as a judge for you in the wink of an eye!
*Then dejectedly.*
But what can you do now, darlin'? You haven't even got him here.

He's down at the Inn sitting alone, drinking and dreaming of the little whores he'll be with tomorrow night on Broadway.

JOSIE

I'll get him here! I'll humble my pride and go down to the Inn for him! And if he doesn't want to come I've a way to make him. I'll raise a scene and pretend I'm in a rage because he forgot his date. I'll disgrace him till he'll be glad to come with me to shut me up. I know his weakness, and it's his vanity about his women. If I was a dainty, pretty tart he'd be proud I'd raise a rumpus about him. But when it's a big, ugly hulk like me—
*She falters and forces herself to go on.*
If he ever was tempted to want me, he'd be ashamed of it. That's the truth behind the lies he told you of his conscience and his fear he might ruin me, God damn him!

HOGAN

No, he meant it, Josie. But never mind that now. Let's say you've got him here. Then what will you do?

JOSIE

I told you this morning if he ever broke his promise to us I'd do any-thing and not mind how crooked it was. And I will! Your part in it is to come at sunrise with witnesses and catch us in—
*She falters.*

HOGAN

In bed, is it? Then it's Mike's second scheme you're thinking about?

JOSIE

I told you I didn't care how dirty a trick—
*With a hard bitter laugh.*
The dirtier the better now!

HOGAN

But how'll you get him in bed, with all his honorable scruples, think-ing you're a virgin? But I'm forgetting he stayed away because he was afraid he'd be tempted. So maybe—

79

JOSIE

*Tensely.*

For the love of God, don't harp on his lies. He won't be tempted at all. But I'll get him so drunk he'll fall asleep and I'll carry him in and put him in bed—

HOGAN

Be God, that's the way! But you'll have to get a pile of whiskey down him. You'll never do it unless you're more sociable and stop looking at him, the way you do, whenever he takes a drink, as if you was praying Almighty God to forgive a poor drunkard. You've got to encourage him. The best way would be for you to drink with him. It would put him at his ease and unsuspecting, and it'd give you courage, too, so you'd act bold for a change instead of giving him brazen talk he's tired of hearing, while you act shy as a mouse.

JOSIE

*Gives her father a bitter, resentful look.*

You're full of sly advice all of a sudden, ain't you? You dirty little tick!

HOGAN

*Angrily.*

Didn't you tell me to get hold of my wits? Be God, if you want me drunk, I've only to let go. That'd suit me. I want to forget my sorrow, and I've no faith in your scheme because you'll be too full of scruples. Like the drinking. You're such a virtuous teetotaller—

JOSIE

I've told you I'd do anything now!

*Then confusedly.*

All I meant was, it's not right, a father to tell his daughter how to—

*Then angrily.*

I don't need your advice. Haven't I had every man I want around here?

HOGAN

Ah, thank God, that sounds natural! Be God, I thought you'd started playing virgin with me just because that Broadway sucker thinks you're one.

JOSIE

*Furiously.*

Shut up! I'm not playing anything. And don't worry I can't do my part of the trick.

HOGAN

That's the talk! But let me get it all clear. I come at sunrise with my witnesses, and you've forgot to lock your door, and we walk in, and there's the two of you in bed, and I raise the roof and threaten him if he don't marry you—

JOSIE

Marry him? After what he's done to us? I wouldn't marry him now if he was the last man on earth! All we want is a paper signed by him with witnesses that he'll sell the farm to you for the price you offered, and not to Harder.

HOGAN

Well, that's justice, but that's all it is. I thought you wanted to make him pay for his black treachery against us, the dirty bastard!

JOSIE

I do want!

*She again gives him a bitter resentful glance.*

It's the estate money you're thinking of, isn't it? Leave it to you!

*Hastily.*

Well, so am I! I'd like to get my hooks on it!

*With a hard, brazen air.*

Be God, if I'm to play whore, I deserve my pay! We'll make him sign a paper he owes me ten thousand dollars the minute the estate is settled.

*She laughs.*

How's that? I'll bet none of his tarts on Broadway ever got a thousandth part of that out of him, no matter how dainty and pretty!

*Laughing again.*

And here's what'll be the greatest joke to teach him a lesson. He'll pay it for nothing! I'll get him in bed but I'll never let him—

HOGAN

*With delighted admiration.*

Och, by Jaysus, Josie, that's the best yet!

*He slaps his thigh enthusiastically.*

Oh, that'll teach him to double-cross his friends! That'll show him two can play at tricks! And him believing you so innocent! Be God, you'll make him the prize sucker of the world! Won't I roar inside me when I see his face in the morning!

*He bursts into coarse laughter.*

JOSIE

*Again with illogical resentment.*

Stop laughing! You're letting yourself be drunk again.

*Then with a hard, business-like air.*

We've done enough talking. Let's start—

HOGAN

Wait, now. There's another thing. Just what do you want me to threaten him with when I catch you? That we'll sue him for outraging your virtue? Sure, his lawyer would have all your old flames in the witness box, till the jury would think you'd been faithful to the male inhabitants of America. So what threat—I can't think of any he wouldn't laugh at.

JOSIE

*Tensely.*

Well, I can! Do I have to tell you his weakness again? It's his vanity about women, and his Broadway pride he's so wise no woman could fool him. It's the disgrace to his vanity—being caught with the likes of me—

*Falteringly, but forcing herself to go on.*

My mug beside his in all the newspapers—the New York papers, too—he'll see the whole of Broadway splitting their sides laughing at him—and he'll give anything to keep us quiet, I tell you. He will! I know him! So don't worry—

*She ends up on the verge of bitter humiliated tears.*

HOGAN

*Without looking at her — enthusiastic again.*
Be God, you're right!

JOSIE

*Gives him a bitter glance — fiercely.*
Then get the hell out of that chair and let's start it!
*He gets up. She surveys him resentfully.*
You're steady on your pins, ain't you, you scheming old thief, now
there's the smell of money around!
*Quickly.*
Well, I'm glad. I know I can depend on you now. You'll walk down
to the Inn with me and hide outside until you see me come out with
him. Then you can sneak in the Inn yourself and pick the witnesses
to stay up with you. But mind you don't get drunk again, and let
them get too drunk.

HOGAN

I won't, I take my oath!
*He pats her on the shoulder approvingly.*
Be God, you've got the proud, fighting spirit in you that never says
die, and you make me ashamed of my weakness. You're that eager
now, be damned if I don't almost think you're glad of the excuse!

JOSIE

*Stiffens.*
Excuse for what, you old —

HOGAN

To show him no man can get the best of you — what else? — like you
showed all the others.

JOSIE

I'll show him to his sorrow!
*Then abruptly, starting for the screen door at left.*
Come on. We've no time to waste.
*But when she gets to the door, she appears suddenly hesitant and timid —
hurriedly.*
Wait. I'd better give a look at myself in the mirror.

*In a brazen tone.*
Sure, those in my trade have to look their best!
*She hurries back across the room into her bedroom and closes the door.*
HOGAN *stares after her. Abruptly he ceases to look like a drunk who, by an effort, is keeping himself half-sober. He is a man who has been drinking a lot but is still clear-headed and has complete control of himself.*

HOGAN
*Watches the crack under* JOSIE's *door and speaks half-aloud to himself, shaking his head pityingly.*
A look in the mirror and she's forgot to light her lamp!
*Remorsefully.*
God forgive me, it's bitter medicine. But it's the only way I can see that has a chance now.

JOSIE's *door opens. At once, he is as he was. She comes out, a fixed smile on her lips, her head high, her face set defiantly. But she has evidently been crying.*

JOSIE
*Brazenly.*
There, now. Don't I look ten thousand dollars' worth to any drunk?

HOGAN
You look a million, darlin'!

JOSIE
*Goes to the screen door and pushes it open with the manner of one who has burned all bridges.*
Come along, then.
*She goes out. He follows close on her heels. She stops abruptly on the first step — startledly.*
Look! There's someone on the road —

HOGAN
*Pushes past her down the steps — peering off left-front — as if aloud to himself, in dismay.*
Be God, it's him! I never thought —

JOSIE
*As if aloud to herself.*
So he didn't forget—

HOGAN
*Quickly.*
Well, it proves he can't keep away from you, and that'll make it easier
for you—
*Then furiously.*
Oh, the dirty, double-crossing bastard! The nerve of him! Coming
to call on you, after making you wait for hours, thinking you don't
know what he's done to us this night, and it'll be a fine cruel joke
to blarney you in the moonlight, and you trusting him like a poor
sheep, and never suspecting—

JOSIE
*Stung.*
Shut up! I'll teach him who's the joker! I'll let him go on as if you
hadn't told me what he's done—

HOGAN
Yes, don't let him suspect it, or you wouldn't fool him. He'd know
you were after revenge. But he can see me here now. I can't sneak
away or he'd be suspicious. We've got to think of a new scheme quick
to get me away—

JOSIE
*Quickly.*
I know how. Pretend you're as drunk as when you came. Make him
believe you're so drunk you don't remember what he's done so he
can't suspect you told me.

HOGAN
I will. Be God, Josie, damned if I don't think he's so queer drunk
himself he don't remember, or he'd never come here.

JOSIE
The drunker he is the better!
*Lowering her voice—quickly.*
He's turned in the gate where he can hear us. Pretend we're fight-

ing and I'm driving you off till you're sober. Say you won't be back tonight. It'll make him sure he'll have the night alone with me. You start the fight.

HOGAN

*Becomes at once very drunk. He shouts.*

Put me out of my own home, will you, you undutiful slut!

JOSIE

Celebration or not, I'll have no drunks cursing and singing all night. Go back to the Inn.

HOGAN

I will! I'll get a room and two bottles and stay drunk as long as I please!

JOSIE

Don't come back till you've slept it off, or I'll wipe the floor with you!

TYRONE *enters, left-front. He does not appear to be drunk—that is, he shows none of the usual symptoms. He seems much the same as in Act One. The only perceptible change is that his eyes have a peculiar fixed, glazed look, and there is a certain vague quality in his manner and speech, as if he were a bit hazy and absent-minded.*

TYRONE

*Dryly.*

Just in time for the Big Bout. Or is this the final round?

HOGAN

*Whirls on him unsteadily.*

Who the hell—

*Peering at him.*

Oh, it's you, is it?

TYRONE

What was the big idea, Phil, leaving me flat?

HOGAN

Leave you flat? Be Jaysus, that reminds me I owe you a swipe on the jaw for something. What was it? Be God, I'm too drunk to remember. But here it is, anyway.

*He turns loose a round-house swing that misses* TYRONE *by a couple of feet, and reels away.* TYRONE *regards him with vague surprise.*

JOSIE

Stop it, you damned old fool, and get out of here!

HOGAN

Taking his side against your poor old father, are you? A hell of a daughter!

*He draws himself up with drunken dignity.*

Don't expect me home tonight, Miss Hogan, or tomorrow either, maybe. You can take your bad temper out on your sweetheart here.

*He starts off down the road, left-front, with a last word over his shoulder.*

Bad luck to you both.

*He disappears. A moment later he begins to bawl his mournful Irish song.*

"Oh, the praties they grow small, Over here, over here," etc.

*During a part of the following scene the song continues to be heard at intervals, receding as he gets farther off on his way to the Inn.*

JOSIE

Well, thank God. That's good riddance.

*She comes to* TYRONE, *who stands staring after* HOGAN *with a puzzled look.*

TYRONE

I've never seen him that stinko before. Must have got him all of a sudden. He didn't seem so lit up at the Inn, but I guess I wasn't paying much attention.

JOSIE

*Forcing a playful air.*

I should think, if you were a real gentleman, you'd be apologizing to me, not thinking of him. Don't you know you're two hours and a half late? I oughtn't to speak to you, if I had any pride.

TYRONE

*Stares at her curiously.*

You've got too damn much pride, Josie. That's the trouble.

JOSIE

And just what do you mean by that, Jim?

TYRONE

*Shrugs his shoulders.*
Nothing. Forget it. I do apologize, Josie. I'm damned sorry. Haven't any excuse. Can't think up a lie.
*Staring at her curiously again.*
Or, now I think of it, I had a damned good honorable excuse, but—
*He shrugs.*
Nuts. Forget it.

JOSIE

Holy Joseph, you're full of riddles tonight. Well, I don't need excuses. I forgive you, anyway, now you're here.
*She takes his hand—playfully.*
Come on now and we'll sit on my bedroom steps and be romantic in the moonlight, like we planned to.
*She leads him there. He goes along in an automatic way, as if only half-conscious of what he is doing. She sits on the top step and pulls him down on the step beneath her. A pause. He stares vaguely at nothing. She bends to give him an uneasy appraising glance.*

TYRONE

*Suddenly, begins to talk mechanically.*
Had to get out of the damned Inn. I was going batty alone there. The old heebie-jeebies. So I came to you.
*He pauses—then adds with strange, wondering sincerity.*
I've really begun to love you a lot, Josie.

JOSIE

*Blurts out bitterly.*
Yes, you've proved that tonight, haven't you?
*Hurriedly regaining her playful tone.*
But never mind. I said I'd forgive you for being so late. So go on about love. I'm all ears.

TYRONE

*As if he hadn't listened.*

I thought you'd have given me up and gone to bed. I remember I had some nutty idea I'd get in bed with you — just to lie with my head on your breast.

JOSIE

*Moved in spite of herself — but keeps her bold, playful tone.*

Well, maybe I'll let you —

*Hurriedly.*

Later on, I mean. The night's young yet, and we'll have it all to ourselves.

*Boldly again.*

But here's for a starter.

*She puts her arms around him and draws him back till his head is on her breast.*

There, now.

TYRONE

*Relaxes — simply and gratefully.*

Thanks, Josie.

*He closes his eyes. For a moment, she forgets everything and stares down at his face with a passionate, possessive tenderness. A pause. From far-off on the road to the Inn,* HOGAN's *mournful song drifts back through the moonlight quiet: "Oh, the praties they grow small, Over here, over here."* TYRONE *rouses himself and straightens up. He acts embarrassed, as if he felt he'd been making a fool of himself — mockingly.*

Hark, Hark, the Donegal lark! "Thou wast not born for death, immortal bird." Can't Phil sing anything but that damned dirge, Josie?

*She doesn't reply. He goes on hazily.*

Still, it seems to belong tonight — in the moonlight — or in my mind —

*He quotes.*

> Now more than ever seems it rich to die,
> To cease upon the midnight with no pain,
> In such an ecstasy!

*He has recited this with deep feeling. Now he sneers.*

Good God! Ode to Phil the Irish Nightingale! I must have the D.T.'s.

JOSIE

*Her face grown bitter.*
Maybe it's only your bad conscience.

TYRONE

*Starts guiltily and turns to stare into her face—suspiciously.*
What put that in your head? Conscience about what?

JOSIE

*Quickly.*
How would I know, if you don't?
*Forcing a playful tone.*
For the sin of wanting to be in bed with me. Maybe that's it.

TYRONE

*With strange relief.*
Oh.
*A bit shamefacedly.*
Forget that stuff, Josie. I was half nutty.

JOSIE

*Bitterly.*
Och, for the love of God, don't apologize as if you was ashamed of—
*She catches herself.*

TYRONE

*With a quick glance at her face.*
All right. I certainly won't apologize—if you're not kicking. I was afraid I might have shocked your modesty.

JOSIE

*Roughly.*
*My* modesty? Be God, I didn't know I had any left.

TYRONE

*Draws away from her—irritably.*
Nix, Josie. Lay off that line, for tonight at least.
*He adds slowly.*
I'd like tonight to be different.

JOSIE

Different from what?

*He doesn't answer. She forces a light tone.*

All right. I'll be as different as you please.

TYRONE

*Simply.*

Thanks, Josie. Just be yourself.

*Again as if he were ashamed, or afraid he had revealed some weakness—off-handedly.*

This being out in the moonlight instead of the lousy Inn isn't a bad bet, at that. I don't know why I hang out in that dump, except I'm even more bored in the so-called good hotels in this hick town.

JOSIE

*Trying to examine his face without his knowing.*

Well, you'll be back on Broadway soon now, won't you?

TYRONE

I hope so.

JOSIE

Then you'll have all the pretty little tarts to comfort you when you get your sorrowful spell on.

TYRONE

Oh, to hell with the rough stuff, Josie! You promised you'd can it tonight.

JOSIE

*Tensely.*

You're a fine one to talk of promises!

TYRONE

*Vaguely surprised by her tone.*

What's the matter? Still sore at me for being late?

JOSIE

*Quickly.*

I'm not. I was teasing you. To prove there's no hard feelings, how would you like a drink? But I needn't ask.

*She gets up.*
I'll get a bottle of his best.

TYRONE
*Mechanically.*
Fine. Maybe that will have some kick. The booze at the Inn didn't work tonight.

JOSIE
Well, this'll work.
*She starts to go into her bedroom. He sits hunched up on the step, staring at nothing. She pauses in the doorway to glance back. The hard, calculating expression on her face softens. For a second she stares at him, bewildered by her conflicting feelings. Then she goes inside, leaving the door open. She opens the door from her room to the lighted living room, and is seen going to the kitchen on the way to the cellar. She has left the door from the living room to her bedroom open and the light reveals a section of the bedroom framed in the doorway behind* TYRONE. *The foot of the bed which occupies most of the room can be seen, and that is all except that the walls are unpainted pine boards.* TYRONE *continues to stare at nothing, but becomes restless. His hands and mouth twitch.*

TYRONE
*Suddenly, with intense hatred.*
You rotten bastard!
*He springs to his feet—fumbles in his pockets for cigarettes—strikes a match which lights up his face, on which there is now an expression of miserable guilt. His hand is trembling so violently he cannot light the cigarette.*

CURTAIN

# Act Three

SCENE

*The living-room wall has been replaced and all we see now of its lighted interior is through the two windows. Otherwise, everything is the same, and this Act follows the preceding without any lapse of time.* TYRONE *is still trying with shaking hands to get his cigarette lighted. Finally he succeeds, and takes a deep inhale, and starts pacing back and forth a few steps, as if in a cell of his own thought. He swears defensively.*

God damn it. You'll be crying in your beer in a minute.

*He begins to sing sneeringly half under his breath a snatch from an old sob song, popular in the Nineties.*

> And baby's cries can't waken her
> In the baggage coach ahead.

*His sneer changes to a look of stricken guilt and grief.*

Christ!

*He seems about to break down and sob but he fights this back.*

Cut it out, you drunken fool!

JOSIE *can be seen through the windows, returning from the kitchen. He turns with a look of relief and escape.*

Thank God!

*He sits on the boulder and waits.* JOSIE *stops by the table in the living room to turn down the lamp until only a dim light remains. She has a quart of whiskey under her arm, two tumblers, and a pitcher of water. She goes through her bedroom and appears in the outer doorway.* TYRONE *gets up.*

Ah! At last the old booze!

*He relieves her of the pitcher and tumblers as she comes down the steps.*

JOSIE
*With a fixed smile.*

You'd think I'd been gone years. You didn't seem so perishing for a drink.

TYRONE
*In his usual, easy, kidding way.*
It's you I was perishing for. I've been dying of loneliness—

JOSIE
You'll die of lying some day. But I'm glad you're alive again. I thought when I left you really were dying on me.

TYRONE
No such luck.

JOSIE
Och, don't talk like that. Come have a drink. We'll use the boulder for a table and I'll be barkeep.
*He puts the pitcher and tumblers on the boulder and she uncorks the bottle. She takes a quick glance at his face—startledly.*
What's come over you, Jim? You look as if you've seen a ghost.

TYRONE
*Looks away—dryly.*
I have. My own. He's punk company.

JOSIE
Yes, it's the worst ghost of all, your own. Don't I know? But this will keep it in its place.
*She pours a tumbler half full of whiskey and hands it to him.*
Here. But wait till I join you.
*She pours the other tumbler half full.*

TYRONE
*Surprised.*
Hello! I thought you never touched it.

JOSIE
*Glibly.*
I have on occasion. And this is one. I don't want to be left out altogether from celebrating our victory over Harder.

*She gives him a sharp bitter glance. Meeting his eyes, which are regarding her with puzzled wonder, she forces a laugh.*

Don't look at me as if I was up to some game. A drink or two will make me better company, and help me enjoy the moon and the night with you. Here's luck.

*She touches his glass with hers.*

TYRONE

*Shrugs his shoulders.*

All right. Here's luck.

*They drink. She gags and sputters. He pours water in her glass. She drinks it. He puts his glass and the pitcher back on the boulder. He keeps staring at her with a puzzled frown.*

JOSIE

Some of it went down the wrong way.

TYRONE

So I see. That'll teach you to pour out baths instead of drinks.

JOSIE

It's the first time I ever heard you complain a drink was too big.

TYRONE

Yours was too big.

JOSIE

I'm my father's daughter. I've a strong head. So don't worry I'll pass out and you'll have to put me to bed.

*She gives a little bold laugh.*

Sure, that's a beautiful notion. I'll have to pretend I'm—

TYRONE

*Irritably.*

Nix on the raw stuff, Josie. Remember you said—

JOSIE

*Resentment in her kidding.*

I'd be different? That's right. I'm forgetting it's your pleasure to have me pretend I'm an innocent virgin tonight.

TYRONE

*In a strange tone that is almost threatening.*
If you don't look out, I'll call you on that bluff, Josie.
*He stares at her with a deliberate sensualist's look that undresses her.*
I'd like to. You know that, don't you?

JOSIE

*Boldly.*
I don't at all. You're the one who's bluffing.

TYRONE

*Grabs her in his arms—with genuine passion.*
Josie!
*Then as suddenly he lets her go.*
Nix. Let's cut it out.
*He turns away. Her face betrays the confused conflict within her of fright, passion, happiness, and bitter resentment. He goes on with an abrupt change of tone.*
How about another drink? That's honest-to-God old bonded Bourbon. How the devil did Phil get hold of it?

JOSIE

Tom Lombardo, the bootlegger, gave him a case for letting him hide a truckload in our barn when the agents were after him. He stole it from a warehouse on faked permits.
*She pours out drinks as she speaks, a half tumblerful for him, a small one for herself.*
Here you are.
*She gives him his drink—smiles at him coquettishly, beginning to show the effect of her big drink by her increasingly bold manner.*
Let's sit down where the moon will be in our eyes and we'll see romance.
*She takes his arm and leads him to her bedroom steps. She sits on the top step, pulling him down beside her but on the one below. She raises her glass.*
Here's hoping before the night's out you'll have more courage and kiss me at least.

TYRONE

*Frowns—then kiddingly.*

That's a promise. Here's how.

*He drains his tumbler. She drinks half of hers. He puts his glass on the ground beside him. A pause. She tries to read his face without his noticing. He seems to be lapsing again into vague preoccupation.*

JOSIE

Now don't sink back half-dead-and-alive in dreams the way you were before.

TYRONE

*Quickly.*

I'm not. I had a good final dose of heebie-jeebies when you were in the house. That's all for tonight.

*He adds a bit maudlinly, his two big drinks beginning to affect him.*

Let the dead past bury its dead.

JOSIE

That's the talk. There's only tonight, and the moon, and us—and the bonded Bourbon. Have another drink, and don't wait for me.

TYRONE

Not now, thanks. They're coming too fast.

*He gives her a curious, cynically amused look.*

Trying to get me soused, Josie?

JOSIE

*Starts—quickly.*

I'm not. Only to get you feeling happy, so you'll forget all sadness.

TYRONE

*Kiddingly.*

I might forget all my honorable intentions, too. So look out.

JOSIE

I'll look forward to it—and I hope that's another promise, like the kiss you owe me. If you're suspicious I'm trying to get you soused— well, here goes.

*She drinks what is left in her glass.*
There, now. I must be scheming to get myself soused, too.

TYRONE
Maybe you are.

JOSIE
*Resentfully.*
If I was, it'd be to make you feel at home. Don't all the pretty little Broadway tarts get soused with you?

TYRONE
*Irritably.*
There you go again with that old line!

JOSIE
All right, I won't!
*Forcing a laugh.*
I must be eaten up with jealousy for them, that's it.

TYRONE
You needn't be. They don't belong.

JOSIE
And I do?

TYRONE
Yes. You do.

JOSIE
For tonight only, you mean?

TYRONE
We've agreed there is only tonight—and it's to be different from any past night—for both of us.

JOSIE
*In a forced, kidding tone.*
I hope it will be. I'll try to control my envy for your Broadway flames. I suppose it's because I have a picture of them in my mind as small and dainty and pretty—

TYRONE
They're just gold-digging tramps.

JOSIE
*As if he hadn't spoken.*
While I'm only a big, rough, ugly cow of a woman.

TYRONE
Shut up! You're beautiful.

JOSIE
*Jeeringly, but her voice trembles.*
God pity the blind!

TYRONE
You're beautiful to me.

JOSIE
It must be the Bourbon—

TYRONE
You're real and healthy and clean and fine and warm and strong and kind—

JOSIE
I have a beautiful soul, you mean?

TYRONE
Well, I don't know much about ladies' souls—
*He takes her hand.*
But I do know you're beautiful.
*He kisses her hand.*
And I love you a lot—in my fashion.

JOSIE
*Stammers.*
Jim—
*Hastily forcing her playful tone.*
Sure, you're full of fine compliments all of a sudden, and I ought to show you how pleased I am.

*She pulls his head back and kisses him on the lips—a quick, shy kiss.*
That's for my beautiful soul.

TYRONE
*The kiss arouses his physical desire. He pulls her head down and stares into her eyes.*
You have a beautiful strong body, too, Josie—and beautiful eyes and hair, and a beautiful smile and beautiful warm breasts.
*He kisses her on the lips. She pulls back frightenedly for a second—then returns his kiss. Suddenly he breaks away—in a tone of guilty irritation.*
Nix! Nix! Don't be a fool, Josie. Don't let me pull that stuff.

JOSIE
*Triumphant for a second.*
You meant it! I know you meant it!
*Then with resentful bitterness—roughly.*
Be God, you're right I'm a damned fool to let you make me forget you're the greatest liar in the world!
*Quickly.*
I mean, the greatest kidder. And now, how about another drink?

TYRONE
*Staring at nothing—vaguely.*
You don't get me, Josie. You don't know—and I hope you never will know—

JOSIE
*Blurts out bitterly.*
Maybe I know more than you think.

TYRONE
*As if she hadn't spoken.*
There's always the aftermath that poisons you. I don't want you to be poisoned—

JOSIE
Maybe you know what you're talking about—

TYRONE
And I don't want to be poisoned myself—not again—not with you.

*He pauses—slowly.*
There have been too many nights—and dawns. This must be different. I want—
*His voice trails off into silence.*

JOSIE
*Trying to read his face—uneasily.*
Don't get in one of your queer spells, now.
*She gives his shoulder a shake—forcing a light tone.*
Sure, I don't think you know what you want. Except another drink. I'm sure you want that. And I want one, too.

TYRONE
*Recovering himself.*
Fine! Grand idea.
*He gets up and brings the bottle from the boulder. He picks up his tumbler and pours a big drink. She is holding out her tumbler but he ignores it.*

JOSIE
You're not polite, pouring your own first.

TYRONE
I said a drink was a grand idea—for me. Not for you. You skip this one.

JOSIE
*Resentfully.*
Oh, I do, do I? Are you giving me orders?

TYRONE
Yes. Take a big drink of moonlight instead.

JOSIE
*Angrily.*
You'll pour me a drink, if you please, Jim Tyrone, or—

TYRONE
*Stares at her—then shrugs his shoulders.*
All right, if you want to take it that way, Josie. It's your funeral.
*He pours a drink into her tumbler.*

JOSIE

*Ashamed but defiant—stiffly.*

Thank you kindly.

*She raises her glass—mockingly.*

Here's to tonight.

TYRONE *is staring at her, a strange bitter disgust in his eyes. Suddenly he slaps at her hand, knocking the glass to the ground.*

TYRONE

*His voice hard with repulsion.*

I've slept with drunken tramps on too many nights!

JOSIE

*Stares at him, too startled and bewildered to be angry. Her voice trembles with surprising meekness.*

All right, Jim, if you don't want me to—

TYRONE

*Now looks as bewildered by his action as she does.*

I'm sorry, Josie. Don't know what the drink got into me.

*He picks up her glass.*

Here. I'll pour you another.

JOSIE

*Still meek.*

No, thank you. I'll skip this one.

*She puts the glass on the ground.*

But you drink up.

TYRONE

Thanks.

*He gulps down his drink. Mechanically, as if he didn't know what he was doing, he pours another. Suddenly he blurts out with guilty loathing.*

That fat blonde pig on the train—I got her drunk! That's why—

*He stops guiltily.*

JOSIE

*Uneasily.*

What are you talking about? What train?

TYRONE

No train. Don't mind me.

*He gulps down the drink and pours another with the same strange air of acting unconsciously.*

Maybe I'll tell you—later, when I'm—That'll cure you—for all time!

*Abruptly he realizes what he is saying. He gives the characteristic shrug of shoulders—cynically.*

Nuts! The Brooklyn boys are talking again. I guess I'm more stewed than I thought—in the center of the old bean, at least.

*Dully.*

I better beat it back to the Inn and go to bed and stop bothering you, Josie.

JOSIE

*Bullyingly—and pityingly.*

Well, you won't, not if I have to hold you. Come on now, bring your drink and sit down like you were before.

*He does so. She pats his cheek—forcing a playful air.*

That's a good boy. And I won't take any more whiskey. I've all the effect from it I want already. Everything is far away and doesn't matter—except the moon and its dreams, and I'm part of the dreams—and you are, too.

*She adds with a rueful little laugh.*

I keep forgetting the thing I've got to remember. I keep hoping it's a lie, even though I know I'm a damned fool.

TYRONE

*Hazily.*

Damned fool about what?

JOSIE

Never mind.

*Forcing a laugh.*

I've just had a thought. If my poor old father had seen you knocking his prize whiskey on the ground—Holy Joseph, he'd have had three paralytic strokes!

TYRONE

*Grins.*

Yes, I can picture him.

*He pauses—with amused affection.*

But that's all a fake. He loves to play tightwad, but the people he likes know better. He'd give them his shirt. He's a grand old scout, Josie.

*A bit maudlin.*

The only real friend I've got left—except you. I love his guts.

JOSIE

*Tensely—sickened by his hypocrisy.*

Och, for the love of God—!

TYRONE

*Shrugs his shoulders.*

Yes, I suppose that does sound like moaning-at-the-bar stuff. But I mean it.

JOSIE

Do you? Well, I know my father's virtues without you telling me.

TYRONE

You ought to appreciate him because he worships the ground you walk on—and he knows you a lot better than you think.

*He turns to smile at her teasingly.*

As well as I do—almost.

JOSIE

*Defensively.*

That's not saying much. Maybe I can guess what you think you know—

*Forcing a contemptuous laugh.*

If it's that, God pity you, you're a terrible fool.

TYRONE

*Teasingly.*

If it's what? I haven't said anything.

JOSIE

You'd better not, or I'll die laughing at you.

*She changes the subject abruptly.*

Why don't you drink up? It makes me nervous watching you hold it as if you didn't know it was there.

TYRONE

I didn't, at that.

*He drinks.*

JOSIE

And have another.

TYRONE

*A bit drunkenly.*

Will a whore go to a picnic? Real bonded Bourbon. That's my dish.

*He goes to the boulder for the bottle. He is as steady on his feet as if he were completely sober.*

JOSIE

*In a light tone.*

Bring the bottle back so it'll be handy and you won't have to leave me. I miss you.

TYRONE

*Comes back with the bottle. He smiles at her cynically.*

Still trying to get me soused, Josie?

JOSIE

I'm not such a fool—with your capacity.

TYRONE

You better watch your step. It might work—and then think of how disgusted you'd feel, with me lying beside you, probably snoring, as you watched the dawn come. You don't know—

JOSIE

*Defiantly.*

The hell I don't! Isn't that the way I've felt with every one of them, after?

TYRONE

*As if he hadn't heard—bitterly.*

But take it from me, I know. I've seen too God-damned many dawns creeping grayly over too many dirty windows.

JOSIE

*Ignores this—boldly.*

But it might be different with you. Love could make it different. And I've been head over heels in love ever since you said you loved my beautiful soul.

*Again he doesn't seem to have heard—resentfully.*

Don't stand there like a loon, mourning over the past. Why don't you pour yourself a drink and sit down?

TYRONE

*Looks at the bottle and tumbler in his hands, as if he'd forgotten them— mechanically.*

Sure thing. Real bonded Bourbon. I ought to know. If I had a dollar for every drink of it I had before Prohibition, I'd hire our dear bully, Harder, for a valet.

JOSIE *stiffens and her face hardens.* TYRONE *pours a drink and sets the bottle on the ground. He looks up suddenly into her eyes—warningly.*

You'd better remember I said you had beautiful eyes and hair—and breasts.

JOSIE

I remember you did.

*She tries to be calculatingly enticing.*

So sit down and I'll let you lay your head—

TYRONE

No. If you won't watch your step, I've got to.

*He sits down but doesn't lean back.*

And don't let me get away with pretending I'm so soused I don't know what I'm doing. I always know. Or part of me does. That's the trouble.

*He pauses—then bursts out in a strange threatening tone.*

You better look out, Josie. She was tickled to death to get me pie-eyed. Had an idea she could roll me, I guess. She wasn't so tickled about it—later on.

JOSIE
What she?
*He doesn't reply. She forces a light tone.*
I hope you don't think I'm scheming to roll you.

TYRONE
*Vaguely.*
What?
*Coming to—indignantly.*
Of course not. What are you talking about? For God's sake, you're not a tart.

JOSIE
*Roughly.*
No, I'm a fool. I'm always giving it away.

TYRONE
*Angrily.*
That lousy bluff again, eh? You're a liar! For Christ sake, quit the smut stuff, can't you!

JOSIE
*Stung.*
Listen to me, Jim! Drunk or not, don't you talk that way to me or—

TYRONE
How about your not talking the old smut stuff to me? You promised you'd be yourself.
*Pauses—vaguely.*
You don't get it, Josie. You see, she was one of the smuttiest talking pigs I've ever listened to.

JOSIE
What she? Do you mean the blonde on the train?

TYRONE
*Starts—sharply.*
Train? Who told you—?

*Quickly.*

Oh—that's right—I did say—

*Vaguely.*

What blonde? What's the difference? Coming back from the Coast. It was long ago. But it seems like tonight. There is no present or future—only the past happening over and over again—now. You can't get away from it.

*Abruptly.*

Nuts! To hell with that crap.

JOSIE

You came back from the Coast about a year ago after—

*She checks herself.*

TYRONE

*Dully.*

Yes. After Mama's death.

*Quickly.*

But I've been to the Coast a lot of times during my career as a third-rate ham. I don't remember which time—or anything much—except I was pie-eyed in a drawing room the whole four days.

*Abruptly.*

What were we talking about before? What a grand guy Phil is. You ought to be glad you've got him for a father. Mine was an old bastard.

JOSIE

He wasn't! He was one of the finest, kindest gentlemen ever lived.

TYRONE

*Sneeringly.*

Outside the family, sure. Inside, he was a lousy tightwad bastard.

JOSIE

*Repelled.*

You ought to be ashamed!

TYRONE

To speak ill of the dead? Nuts! He can't hear, and he knows I hated him, anyway—as much as he hated me. I'm glad he's dead. So is he.

Or he ought to be. Everyone ought to be, if they have any sense. Out of a bum racket. At peace.

*He shrugs his shoulders.*

Nuts! What of it?

JOSIE

*Tensely.*

Don't Jim. I hate you when you talk like that.

*Forcing a light tone.*

Do you want to spoil our beautiful moonlight night? And don't be telling me of your old flames, on trains or not. I'm too jealous.

TYRONE

*With a shudder of disgust.*

Of that pig?

*He drinks his whiskey as if to wash a bad taste from his mouth—then takes one of her hands in both of his—simply.*

You're a fool to be jealous of anyone. You're the only woman I care a damn about.

JOSIE

*Deeply stirred, in spite of herself—her voice trembling.*

Jim, don't—

*Forcing a tense little laugh.*

All right, I'll try and believe that—for tonight.

TYRONE

*Simply.*

Thanks, Josie.

*A pause. He speaks in a tone of random curiosity.*

Why did you say a while ago I'd be leaving for New York soon?

JOSIE

*Stiffens—her face hardening.*

Well, I was right, wasn't I?

*Unconsciously she tries to pull her hand away.*

TYRONE

Why are you pulling your hand away?

JOSIE
*Stops.*
Was I?
*Forcing a smile.*
I suppose because it seems crazy for you to hold my big ugly paw so
tenderly. But you're welcome to it, if you like.

TYRONE
I do like. It's strong and kind and warm—like you.
*He kisses it.*

JOSIE
*Tensely.*
Och, for the love of God—!
*She jerks her hand away—then hastily forces a joking tone.*
Wasting kisses on my hand! Sure, even the moon is laughing at us.

TYRONE
Nuts for the moon! I'd rather have one light on Broadway than all
the moons since Rameses was a pup.
*He takes cigarettes from his pocket and lights one.*

JOSIE
*Her eyes searching his face, lighted up by the match.*
You'll be taking a train back to your dear old Broadway tomorrow
night, won't you?

TYRONE
*Still holding the burning match, stares at her in surprise.*
Tomorrow night? Where did you get that?

JOSIE
A little bird told me.

TYRONE
*Blows out the match in a cloud of smoke.*
You'd better give that bird the bird. By the end of the week, is the
right dope. Phil got his dates mixed.

JOSIE
*Quickly.*
He didn't tell me. He was too drunk to remember anything.

TYRONE
He was sober when I told him. I called up the executors when we reached the Inn after leaving here. They said the estate would be out of probate within a few days. I told Phil the glad tidings and bought drinks for all and sundry. There was quite a celebration. Funny, Phil wouldn't remember that.

JOSIE
*Bewildered — not knowing what to believe.*
It is — funny.

TYRONE
*Shrugs his shoulders.*
Well, he's stewed to the ears. That always explains anything.
*Then strangely.*
Only sometimes it doesn't.

JOSIE
No — sometimes it doesn't.

TYRONE
*Goes on without real interest, talking to keep from thinking.*
Phil certainly has a prize bun on tonight. He never took a punch at me before. And that drivel he talked about owing me one — What got into his head, I wonder.

JOSIE
*Tensely.*
How would I know, if you don't?

TYRONE
Well, I don't. Not unless— I remember I did try to get his goat. Simpson sat down with us. Harder sent him to see me. You remember after Harder left here I said the joke was on you, that you'd made this place a gold mine. I was kidding, but I had the right dope. What

do you think he told Simpson to offer? Ten grand! On the level, Josie.

JOSIE
*Tense.*
So you accepted?

TYRONE
I told Simpson to tell Harder I did. I decided the best way to fix him was to let him think he'd got away with it, and then when he comes tomorrow morning to drive me to the executor's office, I'll tell him what he can do with himself, his bankroll, and tin oil tanks.

JOSIE
*Knows he is telling the truth—so relieved she can only stammer stupidly.*
So that's—the truth of it.

TYRONE
*Smiles.*
Of course, I did it to kid Phil, too. He was right there, listening. But I know I didn't fool him.

JOSIE
*Weakly.*
Maybe you did fool him, for once. But I don't know.

TYRONE
And that's why he took a swing at me?
*He laughs, but there is a forced note to it.*
Well, if so, it's one hell of a joke on him.
*His tone becomes hurt and bitter.*
All the same, I'll be good and sore, Josie. I promised this place wouldn't be sold except to him. What the hell does he think I am? He ought to know I wouldn't double-cross you and him for ten million!

JOSIE
*Giving away at last to her relief and joy.*
Don't I know! Oh, Jim, darling!
*She hugs him passionately and kisses him on the lips.*
I knew you'd never— I told him—

*She kisses him again.*
Oh, Jim, I love you.

TYRONE
*Again with a strange, simple gratitude.*
Thanks, Josie. I mean, for not believing I'm a rotten louse. Everyone else believes it—including myself—for a damned good reason.
*Abruptly changing the subject.*
I'm a fool to let this stuff about Phil get under my skin, but— Why, I remember telling him tonight I'd even written my brother and got his okay on selling the farm to him. And Phil thanked me. He seemed touched and grateful. You wouldn't think he'd forget that.

JOSIE
*Her face hard and bitter.*
I wouldn't, indeed. There's a lot of things he'll have to explain when he comes at sun—
*Hastily.*
When he comes back.
*She pauses—then bursts out.*
The damned old schemer, I'll teach him to—
*Again checking herself.*
to act like a fool.

TYRONE
*Smiles.*
You'll get out the old club, eh? What a bluff you are, Josie.
*Teasingly.*
You and your lovers, Messalina—when you've never—

JOSIE
*With a faint spark of her old defiance.*
You're a liar.

TYRONE
"Pride is the sin by which the angels fell." Are you going to keep that up—with me?

JOSIE
*Feebly.*
You think I've never because no one would—because I'm a great ugly cow—

TYRONE
*Gently.*
Nuts! You could have had any one of them. You kidded them till you were sure they wanted you. That was all you wanted. And then you slapped them groggy when they tried for more. But you had to keep convincing yourself—

JOSIE
*Tormentedly.*
Don't, Jim.

TYRONE
You can take the truth, Josie—from me. Because you and I belong to the same club. We can kid the world but we can't fool ourselves, like most people, no matter what we do—nor escape ourselves no matter where we run away. Whether it's the bottom of a bottle, or a South Sea Island, we'd find our own ghosts there waiting to greet us—"sleepless with pale commemorative eyes," as Rossetti wrote.
*He sneers to himself.*
The old poetic bull, eh? Crap!
*Reverting to a teasing tone.*
You don't ask how I saw through your bluff, Josie. You pretend too much. And so do the guys. I've listened to them at the Inn. They all lie to each other. No one wants to admit all he got was a slap in the puss, when he thinks a lot of other guys made it. You can't blame them. And they know you don't give a damn how they lie. So—

JOSIE
For the love of God, Jim! Don't!

TYRONE
Phil is wise to you, of course, but although he knew I knew, he would never admit it until tonight.

JOSIE

*Startled—vindictively.*
So he admitted it, did he? Wait till I get hold of him!

TYRONE

He'll never admit it to you. He's afraid of hurting you.

JOSIE

He is, is he? Well—
*Almost hysterically.*
For the love of God, can't you shut up about him!

TYRONE

*Glances up at her, surprised—then shrugs his shoulders.*
Oh, all right. I wanted to clear things up, that's all—for Phil's sake
as well as yours. You have a hell of a license to be sore. He's the one
who ought to be. Don't you realize what a lousy position you've put
him in with your brazen-trollop act?

JOSIE

*Tensely.*
No. He doesn't care, except to use me in his scheming. He—

TYRONE

Don't be a damned fool. Of course he cares. And so do I.
*He turns and pulls her head down and kisses her on the lips.*
I care, Josie. I love you.

JOSIE

*With pitiful longing.*
Do you, Jim? Do you?
*She forces a trembling smile—faintly.*
Then I'll confess the truth to you. I've been a crazy fool. I am a vir-
gin.
*She begins to sob with a strange forlorn shame and humiliation.*
And now you'll never—and I want you to—now more than ever—
because I love you more than ever, after what's happened—
*Suddenly she kisses him with fierce passion.*
But you will! I'll make you! To hell with your honorable scruples! I

know you want me! I couldn't believe that until tonight—but now I know. It's in your kisses!

*She kisses him again—with passionate tenderness.*

Oh, you great fool! As if I gave a damn what happened after! I'll have had tonight and your love to remember for the rest of my days!

*She kisses him again.*

Oh, Jim darling, haven't you said yourself there's only tonight?

*She whispers tenderly.*

Come. Come with me.

*She gets to her feet, pulling at his arm—with a little self-mocking laugh.*

But I'll have to make you leave before sunrise. I mustn't forget that.

TYRONE

*A strange change has come over his face. He looks her over now with a sneering cynical lust. He speaks thickly as if he was suddenly very drunk.*

Sure thing, Kiddo. What the hell else do you suppose I came for? I've been kidding myself.

*He steps up beside her and puts his arm around her and presses his body to hers.*

You're the goods, Kid. I've wanted you all along. Love, nuts! I'll show you what love is. I know what you want, Bright Eyes.

*She is staring at him now with a look of frightened horror. He kisses her roughly.*

Come on, Baby Doll, let's hit the hay.

*He pushes her back in the doorway.*

JOSIE

*Strickenly.*

Jim! Don't!

*She pulls his arms away so violently that he staggers back and would fall down the steps if she didn't grab his arm in time. As it is he goes down on one knee. She is on the verge of collapse herself—brokenly.*

Jim! I'm not a whore.

TYRONE

*Remains on one knee—confusedly, as if he didn't know what had happened.*

What the hell? Was I trying to rape you, Josie? Forget it. I'm drunk—not responsible.

*He gets to his feet, staggering a bit, and steps down to the ground.*

JOSIE

*Covering her face with her hands.*

Oh, Jim!

*She sobs.*

TYRONE

*With vague pity.*

Don't cry. No harm done. You stopped me, didn't you?

*She continues to sob. He mutters vaguely, as if talking to himself.*

Must have drawn a blank for a while. Nuts! Cut out the faking. I knew what I was doing.

*Slowly, staring before him.*

But it's funny. I *was* seeing things. That's the truth, Josie. For a moment I thought you were that blonde pig—

*Hastily.*

The old heebie-jeebies. Hair of the dog.

*He gropes around for the bottle and his glass.*

I'll have another shot—

JOSIE

*Takes her hands from her face—fiercely.*

Pour the whole bottle down your throat, if you like! Only stop talking!

*She covers her face with her hands and sobs again.*

TYRONE

*Stares at her with a hurt and sad expression—dully.*

Can't forgive me, eh? You ought to. You ought to thank me for letting you see—

*He pauses, as if waiting for her to say something but she remains silent. He shrugs his shoulders, pours out a big drink mechanically.*

Well, here's how.

*He drinks and puts the bottle and glass on the ground—dully.*

That was a nightcap. Our moonlight romance seems to be a flop, Josie. I guess I'd better go.

JOSIE
*Dully.*
Yes. You'd better go. Good night.

TYRONE
Not good night. Good-bye.

JOSIE
*Lifts her head.*
Good-bye?

TYRONE
Yes. I won't see you again before I leave for New York. I was a damned fool to come tonight. I hoped— But you don't get it. How could you? So what's the good—
*He shrugs his shoulders hopelessly and turns toward the road.*

JOSIE
Jim!

TYRONE
*Turning back—bitter accusation in his tone now.*
Whore? Who said you were a whore? But I warned you, didn't I, if you kept on— Why did you have to act like one, asking me to come to bed? That wasn't what I came here for. And you promised tonight would be different. Why the hell did you promise that, if all you wanted was what all the others want, if that's all love means to you?
*Then guiltily.*
Oh, Christ, I don't mean that, Josie. I know how you feel, and if I could give you happiness— But it wouldn't work. You don't know me. I'd poison it for myself and for you. I've poisoned it already, haven't I, but it would be a million times worse after— No matter how I tried not to, I'd make it like all the other nights—for you, too. You'd lie awake and watch the dawn come with disgust, with nausea retching your memory, and the wine of passion poets blab about, a sour aftertaste in your mouth of Dago red ink!
*He gives a sneering laugh.*

JOSIE
*Distractedly.*
Oh, Jim, don't! Please don't!

TYRONE
You'd hate me and yourself—not for a day or two but for the rest of your life.
*With a perverse, jeering note of vindictive boastfulness in his tone.*
Believe me, Kid, when I poison them, they stay poisoned!

JOSIE
*With dull bitterness.*
Good-bye, Jim.

TYRONE
*Miserably hurt and sad for a second—appealingly.*
Josie—
*Gives the characteristic shrug of his shoulders—simply.*
Good-bye.
*He turns toward the road—bitterly.*
I'll find it hard to forgive, too. I came here asking for love—just for this one night, because I thought you loved me.
*Dully.*
Nuts. To hell with it.
*He starts away.*

JOSIE
*Watches him for a second, fighting the love that, in spite of her, responds to his appeal—then she springs up and runs to him—with fierce, possessive, maternal tenderness.*
Come here to me, you great fool, and stop your silly blather. There's nothing to hate you for. There's nothing to forgive. Sure, I was only trying to give you happiness, because I love. I'm sorry I was so stupid and didn't see— But I see now, and you'll find I have all the love you need.
*She gives him a hug and kisses him. There is passion in her kiss but it is a tender, protective maternal passion, which he responds to with an instant grateful yielding.*

TYRONE

*Simply.*

Thanks, Josie. You're beautiful. I love you. I knew you'd understand.

JOSIE

Of course I do. Come, now.

*She leads him back, her arm around his waist.*

TYRONE

I didn't want to leave you. You know that.

JOSIE

Indeed I know it. Come now. We'll sit down.

*She sits on the top step and pulls him down on the step below her.*

That's it—with my arm around you. Now lay your head on my breast—the way you said you wanted to do—

*He lets his head fall back on her breast. She hugs him—gently.*

There, now. Forget all about my being a fool and forgive—

*Her voice trembles—but she goes on determinedly.*

Forgive my selfishness, thinking only of myself. Sure, if there's one thing I owe you tonight, after all my lying and scheming, it's to give you the love you need, and it'll be my pride and my joy—

*Forcing a trembling echo of her playful tone.*

It's easy enough, too, for I have all kinds of love for you—and maybe this is the greatest of all—because it costs so much.

*She pauses, looking down at his face. He has closed his eyes and his haggard, dissipated face looks like a pale mask in the moonlight—at peace as a death mask is at peace. She becomes frightened.*

Jim! Don't look like that!

TYRONE

*Opens his eyes—vaguely.*

Like what?

JOSIE

*Quickly.*

It's the moonlight. It makes you look so pale, and with your eyes closed—

TYRONE

*Simply.*

You mean I looked dead?

JOSIE

No! As if you'd fallen asleep.

TYRONE

*Speaks in a tired, empty tone, as if he felt he ought to explain something to her—something which no longer interests him.*

Listen, and I'll tell you a little story, Josie. All my life I had just one dream. From the time I was a kid, I loved racehorses. I thought they were the most beautiful things in the world. I liked to gamble, too. So the big dream was that some day I'd have enough dough to play a cagey system of betting on favorites, and follow the horses south in the winter, and come back north with them in the spring, and be at the track every day. It seemed that would be the ideal life—for me.

*He pauses.*

JOSIE

Well, you'll be able to do it.

TYRONE

No. I won't be able to do it, Josie. That's the joke. I gave it a try-out before I came up here. I borrowed some money on my share of the estate, and started going to tracks. But it didn't work. I played my system, but I found I didn't care if I won or lost. The horses were beautiful, but I found myself saying to myself, what of it? Their beauty didn't mean anything. I found that every day I was glad when the last race was over, and I could go back to the hotel—and the bottle in my room.

*He pauses, staring into the moonlight with vacant eyes.*

JOSIE

*Uneasily.*

Why did you tell me this?

TYRONE

*In the same listless monotone.*

You said I looked dead. Well, I am.

JOSIE
You're not!
*She hugs him protectively.*
Don't talk like that!

TYRONE
Ever since Mama died.

JOSIE
*Deeply moved—pityingly.*
I know. I've felt all along it was that sorrow was making you—
*She pauses—gently.*
Maybe if you talked about your grief for her, it would help you. I
think it must be all choked up inside you, killing you.

TYRONE
*In a strange warning tone.*
You'd better look out, Josie.

JOSIE
Why?

TYRONE
*Quickly, forcing his cynical smile.*
I might develop a crying jag, and sob on your beautiful breast.

JOSIE
*Gently.*
You can sob all you like.

TYRONE
Don't encourage me. You'd be sorry.
*A deep conflict shows in his expression and tone. He is driven to go on in
spite of himself.*
But if you're such a glutton for punishment— After all, I said I'd tell
you later, didn't I?

JOSIE
*Puzzled.*
You said you'd tell me about the blonde on the train.

**TYRONE**

She's part of it. I lied about that.

*He pauses—then blurts out sneeringly.*

You won't believe it could have happened. Or if you did believe, you couldn't understand or forgive—

*Quickly.*

But you might. You're the one person who might. Because you really love me. And because you're the only woman I've ever met who understands the lousy rotten things a man can do when he's crazy drunk, and draws a blank—especially when he's nutty with grief to start with.

**JOSIE**

*Hugging him tenderly.*

Of course I'll understand, Jim, darling.

**TYRONE**

*Stares into the moonlight—hauntedly.*

But I didn't draw a blank. I tried to. I drank enough to knock out ten men. But it didn't work. I knew what I was doing.

*He pauses—dully.*

No, I can't tell you, Josie. You'd loathe my guts, and I couldn't blame you.

**JOSIE**

No! I'll love you no matter what—

**TYRONE**

*With strange triumphant harshness.*

All right! Remember that's a promise!

*He pauses—starts to speak—pauses again.*

**JOSIE**

*Pityingly.*

Maybe you'd better not—if it will make you suffer.

**TYRONE**

Trying to welch now, eh? It's too late. You've got me started. Suffer? Christ, I ought to suffer!

*He pauses. Then he closes his eyes. It is as if he had to hide from sight before he can begin. He makes his face expressionless. His voice becomes impersonal and objective, as though what he told concerned some man he had known, but had nothing to do with him. This is the only way he can start telling the story.*

When Mama died, I'd been on the wagon for nearly two years. Not even a glass of beer. Honestly. And I know I would have stayed on. For her sake. She had no one but me. The Old Man was dead. My brother had married—had a kid—had his own life to live. She'd lost him. She had only me to attend to things for her and take care of her. She'd always hated my drinking. So I quit. It made me happy to do it. For her. Because she was all I had, all I cared about. Because I loved her.

*He pauses.*

No one would believe that now, who knew— But I did.

JOSIE
*Gently.*
I know how much you loved her.

TYRONE
We went out to the Coast to see about selling a piece of property the Old Man had bought three years ago. And one day she suddenly became ill. Got rapidly worse. Went into a coma. Brain tumor. The docs said, no hope. Might never come out of coma. I went crazy. Couldn't face losing her. The old booze yen got me. I got drunk and stayed drunk. And I began hoping she'd never come out of the coma, and see I was drinking again. That was my excuse, too—that she'd never know. And she never did.

*He pauses—then sneeringly.*

Nix! Kidding myself again. I know damned well just before she died she recognized me. She saw I was drunk. Then she closed her eyes so she couldn't see, and was glad to die!

*He opens his eyes and stares into the moonlight as if he saw this deathbed scene before him.*

JOSIE
*Soothingly.*
Ssshh. You only imagine that because you feel guilty about drinking.

TYRONE

*As if he hadn't heard, closes his eyes again.*

After that, I kept so drunk I did draw a blank most of the time, but I went through the necessary motions and no one guessed how drunk—

*He pauses.*

But there are things I can never forget—the undertakers, and her body in a coffin with her face made up. I couldn't hardly recognize her. She looked young and pretty like someone I remembered meeting long ago. Practically a stranger. To whom I was a stranger. Cold and indifferent. Not worried about me any more. Free at last. Free from worry. From pain. From me. I stood looking down at her, and something happened to me. I found I couldn't feel anything. I knew I ought to be heartbroken but I couldn't feel anything. I seemed dead, too. I knew I ought to cry. Even a crying jag would look better than just standing there. But I couldn't cry. I cursed to myself, "You dirty bastard, it's Mama. You loved her, and now she's dead. She's gone away from you forever. Never, never again—" But it had no effect. All I did was try to explain to myself, "She's dead. What does she care now if I cry or not, or what I do? It doesn't matter a damn to her. She's happy to be where I can't hurt her ever again. She's rid of me at last. For God's sake, can't you leave her alone even now? For God's sake, can't you let her rest in peace?"

*He pauses—then sneeringly.*

But there were several people around and I knew they expected me to show something. Once a ham, always a ham! So I put on an act. I flopped on my knees and hid my face in my hands and faked some sobs and cried, "Mama! Mama! My dear mother!" But all the time I kept saying to myself, "You lousy ham! You God-damned lousy ham! Christ, in a minute you'll start singing 'Mother Macree'!"

*He opens his eyes and gives a tortured, sneering laugh, staring into the moonlight.*

JOSIE

*Horrified, but still deeply pitying.*

Jim! Don't! It's past. You've punished yourself. And you were drunk. You didn't mean—

TYRONE

*Again closes his eyes.*

I had to bring her body East to be buried beside the Old Man. I took a drawing room and hid in it with a case of booze. She was in her coffin in the baggage car. No matter how drunk I got, I couldn't forget that for a minute. I found I couldn't stay alone in the drawing room. It became haunted. I was going crazy. I had to go out and wander up and down the train looking for company. I made such a public nuisance of myself that the conductor threatened if I didn't quit, he'd keep me locked in the drawing room. But I'd spotted one passenger who was used to drunks and could pretend to like them, if there was enough dough in it. She had parlor house written all over her—a blonde pig who looked more like a whore than twenty-five whores, with a face like an overgrown doll's and a come-on smile as cold as a polar bear's feet. I bribed the porter to take a message to her and that night she sneaked into my drawing room. She was bound for New York, too. So every night—for fifty bucks a night—

*He opens his eyes and now he stares torturedly through the moonlight into the drawing room.*

JOSIE

*Her face full of revulsion—stammers.*

Oh, how could you!

*Instinctively she draws away, taking her arms from around him.*

TYRONE

How could I? I don't know. But I did. I suppose I had some mad idea she could make me forget—what was in the baggage car ahead.

JOSIE

Don't.

*She draws back again so he has to raise his head from her breast. He doesn't seem to notice this.*

TYRONE

No, it couldn't have been that. Because I didn't seem to want to forget. It was like some plot I had to carry out. The blonde—she didn't matter. She was only something that belonged in the plot. It was as if I wanted revenge—because I'd been left alone—because I knew I was lost, without any hope left—that all I could do would be drink myself to death, because no one was left who could help me.

*His face hardens and a look of cruel vindictiveness comes into it—with a strange horrible satisfaction in his tone.*

No, I didn't forget even in that pig's arms! I remembered the last two lines of a lousy tear-jerker song I'd heard when I was a kid kept singing over and over in my brain.

*And baby's cries can't waken her*
*In the baggage coach ahead.*

JOSIE
*Distractedly.*
Jim!

TYRONE
I couldn't stop it singing. I didn't want to stop it!

JOSIE
Jim! For the love of God. I don't want to hear!

TYRONE
*After a pause—dully.*
Well, that's all—except I was too drunk to go to her funeral.

JOSIE
Oh!
*She has drawn away from him as far as she can without getting up. He becomes aware of this for the first time and turns slowly to stare at her.*

TYRONE
*Dully.*
Don't want to touch me now, eh?
*He shrugs his shoulders mechanically.*
Sorry. I'm a damned fool. I shouldn't have told you.

JOSIE
*Her horror ebbing as her love and protective compassion return—moves nearer him—haltingly.*
Don't Jim. Don't say—I don't want to touch you. It's—a lie.
*She puts a hand on his shoulder.*

127

TYRONE

*As if she hadn't spoken—with hopeless longing.*

Wish I could believe in the spiritualists' bunk. If I could tell her it was because I missed her so much and couldn't forgive her for leaving me—

JOSIE

Jim! For the love of God—!

TYRONE

*Unheeding.*

She'd understand and forgive me, don't you think? She always did. She was simple and kind and pure of heart. She was beautiful. You're like her deep in your heart. That's why I told you. I thought—

*Abruptly his expression becomes sneering and cynical—harshly.*

My mistake. Nuts! Forget it. Time I got a move on. I don't like your damned moon, Josie. It's an ad for the past.

*He recites mockingly.*

> It is the very error of the moon:
> She comes more nearer earth than she was wont,
> And makes men mad.

*He moves.*

I'll grab the last trolley for town. There'll be a speak open, and some drunk laughing. I need a laugh.

*He starts to get up.*

JOSIE

*Throws her arms around him and pulls him back—tensely.*

No! You won't go! I won't let you!

*She hugs him close—gently.*

I understand now, Jim, darling, and I'm proud you came to me as the one in the world you know loves you enough to understand and forgive—and I do forgive!

TYRONE

*Lets his head fall back on her breast—simply.*

Thanks, Josie. I know you—

JOSIE

As *she* forgives, do you hear me! As *she* loves and understands and forgives!

TYRONE

*Simply.*
Yes, I know she—
*His voice breaks.*

JOSIE

*Bends over him with a brooding maternal tenderness.*
That's right. Do what you came for, my darling. It isn't drunken laughter in a speakeasy you want to hear at all, but the sound of yourself crying your heart's repentance against her breast.
*His face is convulsed. He hides it on her breast and sobs rackingly. She hugs him more tightly and speaks softly, staring into the moonlight.*
*She* hears. I feel her in the moonlight, her soul wrapped in it like a silver mantle, and I know she understands and forgives me, too, and her blessing lies on me.
*A pause. His sobs begin to stop exhaustedly. She looks down at him again and speaks soothingly as she would to a child.*
There. There, now.
*He stops. She goes on in a gentle, bullying tone.*
You're a fine one, wanting to leave me when the night I promised I'd give you has just begun, our night that'll be different from all the others, with a dawn that won't creep over dirty windowpanes but will wake in the sky like a promise of God's peace in the soul's dark sadness.
*She smiles a little amused smile.*
Will you listen to me, Jim! I must be a poet. Who would have guessed it? Sure, love is a wonderful mad inspiration!
*A pause. She looks down. His eyes are closed. His face against her breast looks pale and haggard in the moonlight. Calm with the drained, exhausted peace of death. For a second she is frightened. Then she realizes and whispers softly.*
Asleep.
*In a tender crooning tone like a lullaby.*
That's right. Sleep in peace, my darling.

*Then with sudden anguished longing.*

Oh, Jim, Jim, maybe my love could still save you, if you could want it enough!

*She shakes her head.*

No. That can never be.

*Her eyes leave his face to stare up at the sky. She looks weary and stricken and sad. She forces a defensive, self-derisive smile.*

God forgive me, it's a fine end to all my scheming, to sit here with the dead hugged to my breast, and the silly mug of the moon grinning down, enjoying the joke!

CURTAIN

# Act Four

*Same as Act Three. It is dawn. The first faint streaks of color, heralding the sunrise, appear in the eastern sky at left.*

JOSIE *sits in the same position on the steps, as if she had not moved, her arms around* TYRONE. *He is still asleep, his head on her breast. His face has the same exhausted, deathlike repose.* JOSIE's *face is set in an expression of numbed, resigned sadness. Her body sags tiredly. In spite of her strength, holding herself like this for hours, for fear of waking him, is becoming too much for her.*

*The two make a strangely tragic picture in the wan dawn light—this big sorrowful woman hugging a haggard-faced, middle-aged drunkard against her breast, as if he were a sick child.*

HOGAN *appears at left-rear, coming from the barn. He approaches the corner of the house stealthily on tiptoe. Wisps of hay stick to his clothes and his face is swollen and sleepy, but his little pig's eyes are sharply wide awake and sober. He peeks around the corner, and takes in the two on the steps. His eyes fix on* JOSIE's *face in a long, probing stare.*

JOSIE
*Speaks in a low grim tone.*
Stop hiding, Father. I heard you sneak up.
*He comes guiltily around the corner. She keeps her voice low, but her tone is commanding.*
Come here, and be quiet about it.
*He obeys meekly, coming as far as the boulder silently, his eyes searching*

her face, his expression becoming guilty and miserable at what he sees.
*She goes on in the same tone, without looking at him.*
Talk low, now. I don't want him wakened—
*She adds strangely.*
Not until the dawn has beauty in it.

HOGAN
*Worriedly.*
What?
*He decides it's better for the present to ask no questions. His eyes fall on*
TYRONE'S *face. In spite of himself, he is startled—in an awed, almost
frightened whisper.*
Be God, he looks dead!

JOSIE
*Strangely.*
Why wouldn't he? He is.

HOGAN
Is?

JOSIE
Don't be a fool. Can't you see him breathing? Dead asleep, I mean.
Don't stand there gawking. Sit down.
*He sits meekly on the boulder. His face betrays a guilty dread of what is
coming. There is a pause in which she doesn't look at him but, he keeps
glancing at her, growing visibly more uneasy. She speaks bitterly.*
Where's your witnesses?

HOGAN
*Guiltily.*
Witnesses?
*Then forcing an amused grin.*
Oh, be God, if that ain't a joke on me! Sure, I got so blind drunk at
the Inn I forgot all about our scheme and came home and went to
sleep in the hayloft.

JOSIE
*Her expression harder and more bitter.*
You're a liar.

HOGAN

I'm not. I just woke up. Look at the hay sticking to me. That's proof.

JOSIE

I'm not thinking of that, and well you know it.
*With bitter voice.*
So you just woke up—did you?—and then came sneaking here to see if the scheme behind your scheme had worked!

HOGAN
*Guiltily.*
I don't know what you mean.

JOSIE

Don't lie any more, Father. This time, you've told one too many.
*He starts to defend himself but the look on her face makes him think better of it and he remains uneasily silent. A pause.*

HOGAN
*Finally has to blurt out.*
Sure, if I'd brought the witnesses, there's nothing for them to witness that—

JOSIE

No. You're right, there. There's nothing. Nothing at all.
*She smiles strangely.*
Except a great miracle they'd never believe, or you either.

HOGAN

What miracle?

JOSIE

A virgin who bears a dead child in the night, and the dawn finds her still a virgin. If that isn't a miracle, what is?

HOGAN
*Uneasily.*
Stop talking so queer. You give me the shivers.
*He attempts a joking tone.*
Is it you who's the virgin? Faith, that *would* be a miracle, no less!
*He forces a chuckle.*

**JOSIE**
I told you to stop lying, Father.

**HOGAN**
What lie?
*He stops and watches her face worriedly. She is silent, as if she were not aware of him now. Her eyes are fixed on the wanton sky.*

**JOSIE**
*As if to herself.*
It'll be beautiful soon, and I can wake him.

**HOGAN**
*Can't retain his anxiety any longer.*
Josie, darlin'! For the love of God, can't you tell me what happened to you?

**JOSIE**
*Her face hard and bitter again.*
I've told you once. Nothing.

**HOGAN**
Nothing? If you could see the sadness in your face—

**JOSIE**
What woman doesn't sorrow for the man she loved who has died? But there's pride in my heart, too.

**HOGAN**
*Tormentedly.*
Will you stop talking as if you'd gone mad in the night!
*Raising his voice—with revengeful anger.*
Listen to me! If Jim Tyrone has done anything to bring you sorrow—
**TYRONE** *stirs in his sleep and moans, pressing his face against her breast as if for protection. She looks down at him and hugs him close.*

**JOSIE**
*Croons softly.*
There, there, my darling. Rest in peace a while longer.
*Turns on her father angrily and whispers.*
Didn't I tell you to speak low and not wake him!

*She pauses—then quietly.*

He did nothing to bring me sorrow. It was my mistake. I thought there was still hope. I didn't know he'd died already—that it was a damned soul coming to me in the moonlight, to confess and be forgiven and find peace for a night—

HOGAN
Josie! Will you stop!

JOSIE
*After a pause—dully.*
He'd never do anything to hurt me. You know it.
*Self-mockingly.*
Sure, hasn't he told me I'm beautiful to him and he loves me—in his fashion.
*Then matter-of-factly.*
All that happened was that he got drunk and he had one of his crazy notions he wanted to sleep the way he is, and I let him sleep.
*With forced roughness.*
And, be God, the night's over. I'm half dead with tiredness and sleepiness. It's that you see in my face, not sorrow.

HOGAN
Don't try to fool me, Josie. I—

JOSIE
*Her face hard and bitter—grimly.*
Fool you, is it? It's you who made a fool of me with your lies, thinking you'd use me to get your dirty greasy paws on the money he'll have!

HOGAN
No! I swear by all the saints—

JOSIE
You'd swear on a Bible while you were stealing it!
*Grimly.*
Listen to me, Father. I didn't call you here to answer questions about what's none of your business. I called you here to tell you I've seen through all the lies you told last night to get me to—

*As he starts to speak.*
Shut up! I'll do the talking now. You weren't drunk. You were only putting it on as part of your scheme—

HOGAN
*Quietly.*
I wasn't drunk, no. I admit that, Josie. But I'd had slews of drinks and they were in my head or I'd never have the crazy dreams—

JOSIE
*With biting scorn.*
Dreams, is it? The only dream you've ever had, or will have, is of yourself counting a fistful of dirty money, and divil a care how you got it, or who you robbed or made suffer!

HOGAN
*Winces—pleadingly.*
Josie!

JOSIE
Shut up.
*Scathingly.*
I'm sure you've made up a whole new set of lies and excuses. You're that cunning and clever, but you can save your breath. They wouldn't fool me now. I've been fooled once too often.
*He gives her a frightened look, as if something he had dreaded has happened. She goes on, grimly accusing.*
You lied about Jim selling the farm. You knew he was kidding. You knew the estate would be out of probate in a few days, and he'd go back to Broadway, and you had to do something quick or you'd lose the last chance of getting your greedy hooks on his money.

HOGAN
*Miserably.*
No. It wasn't that, Josie.

JOSIE
You saw how hurt and angry I was because he'd kept me waiting here, and you used that. You knew I loved him and wanted him and you used that. You used all you knew about me— Oh, you did it clever!

You ought to be proud! You worked it so it was me who did all the dirty scheming— You knew I'd find out from Jim you'd lied about the farm, but not before your lie had done its work—made me go after him, get him drunk, get drunk myself so I could be shameless—and when the truth did come out, wouldn't it make me love him all the more and be more shameless and willing? Don't tell me you didn't count on that, and you such a clever schemer! And if he once had me, knowing I was a virgin, didn't you count on his honor and remorse, and his loving me in his fashion, to make him offer to marry me? Sure, why wouldn't he, you thought. It wouldn't hold him. He'd go back to Broadway just the same and never see me again. But there'd be money in it, and when he'd finished killing himself, I'd be his legal widow and get what's left.

HOGAN
*Miserably.*
No! It wasn't that.

JOSIE
But what's the good of talking? It's all over. I've only one more word for you, Father, and it's this: I'm leaving you today, like my brothers left. You can live alone and work alone your cunning schemes on yourself.

HOGAN
*After a pause—slowly.*
I knew you'd be bitter against me, Josie, but I took the chance you'd be so happy you wouldn't care how—

JOSIE
*As if she hadn't heard, looking at the eastern sky which is now glowing with color.*
Thank God, it's beautiful. It's time.
*To* HOGAN.
Go in the house and stay there till he's gone. I don't want you around to start some new scheme.
*He looks miserable, starts to speak, thinks better of it, and meekly tiptoes past her up the steps and goes in, closing the door quietly after him. She*

*looks down at* TYRONE. *Her face softens with a maternal tenderness—sadly.*

I hate to bring you back to life, Jim, darling. If you could have died in your sleep, that's what you would have liked, isn't it?

*She gives him a gentle shake.*

Wake up, Jim.

*He moans in his sleep and presses more closely against her. She stares at his face.*

Dear God, let him remember that one thing and forget the rest. That will be enough for me.

*She gives him a more vigorous shake.*

Jim! Wake up, do you hear? It's time.

TYRONE

*Half wakens without opening his eyes—mutters.*

What the hell?

*Dimly conscious of a woman's body—cynically.*

Again, eh? Same old stuff. Who the hell are you, sweetheart?

*Irritably.*

What's the big idea, waking me up? What time is it?

JOSIE

It's dawn.

TYRONE

*Still without opening his eyes.*

Dawn?

*He quotes drowsily.*

But I was desolate and sick of an old passion,
When I awoke and found the dawn was gray.

*Then with a sneer.*

They're all gray. Go to sleep, Kid—and let me sleep.

*He falls asleep again.*

JOSIE

*Tensely.*

This one isn't gray, Jim. It's different from all the others—

*She sees he is asleep—bitterly.*

He'll have forgotten. He'll never notice. And I'm the whore on the train to him now, not—
*Suddenly she pushes him away from her and shakes him roughly.*
Will you wake up, for God's sake! I've had all I can bear—

TYRONE
*Still half asleep.*
Hey! Cut out the rough stuff, Kid. What?
*Awake now, blinking his eyes—with dazed surprise.*
Josie.

JOSIE
*Still bitter.*
That's who, and none of your damned tarts!
*She pushes him.*
Get up now, so you won't fall asleep again.
*He does so with difficulty, still in a sleepy daze, his body stiff and cramped. She conquers her bitter resentment and puts on her old free-and-easy kidding tone with him, but all the time waiting to see how much he will remember.*
You're stiff and cramped, and no wonder. I'm worse from holding you, if that's any comfort.
*She stretches and rubs her numbed arms, groaning comically.*
Holy Joseph, I'm a wreck entirely. I'll never be the same.
*Giving him a quick glance.*
You look as if you'd drawn a blank and were wondering how you got here. I'll bet you don't remember a thing.

TYRONE
*Moving his arms and legs gingerly—sleepily.*
I don't know. Wait till I'm sure I'm still alive.

JOSIE
You need an eye-opener.
*She picks up the bottle and glass and pours him a drink.*
Here you are.

TYRONE
*Takes the glass mechanically.*

Thanks, Josie.

*He goes and sits on the boulder, holding the drink as if he had no interest in it.*

JOSIE

*Watching him.*

Drink up or you'll be asleep again.

TYRONE

No, I'm awake now, Josie. Funny. Don't seem to want a drink. Oh, I've got a head all right. But no heebie-jeebies—yet.

JOSIE

That's fine. It must be a pleasant change—

TYRONE

It is. I've got a nice, dreamy peaceful hangover for once—as if I'd had a sound sleep without nightmares.

JOSIE

So you did. Divil a nightmare. I ought to know. Wasn't I holding you and keeping them away?

TYRONE

You mean you—

*Suddenly.*

Wait a minute. I remember now I was sitting alone at a table in the Inn, and I suddenly had a crazy notion I'd come up here and sleep with my head on your— So that's why I woke up in your arms.

*Shamefacedly.*

And you let me get away with it. You're a nut, Josie.

JOSIE

Oh, I didn't mind.

TYRONE

You must have seen how blotto I was, didn't you?

JOSIE

I did. You were as full as a tick.

**TYRONE**

Then why didn't you give me the bum's rush?

**JOSIE**

Why would I? I was glad to humor you.

**TYRONE**

For God's sake, how long was I cramped on you like that?

**JOSIE**

Oh, a few hours, only.

**TYRONE**

God, I'm sorry Josie, but it's your own fault for letting me—

**JOSIE**

Och, don't be apologizing. I was glad of the excuse to stay awake and enjoy the beauty of the moon.

**TYRONE**

Yes, I can remember what a beautiful night it was.

**JOSIE**

Can you? I'm glad of that, Jim. You seemed to enjoy it the while we were sitting here together before you fell asleep.

**TYRONE**

How long a while was that?

**JOSIE**

Not long. Less than an hour, anyway.

**TYRONE**

I suppose I bored the hell out of you with a lot of drunken drivel.

**JOSIE**

Not a lot, no. But some. You were full of blarney, saying how beautiful I was to you.

**TYRONE**
*Earnestly.*
That wasn't drivel, Josie. You were. You are. You always will be.

**JOSIE**

You're a wonder, Jim. Nothing can stop you, can it? Even me in the light of dawn, looking like something you'd put in the field to scare the crows from the corn. You'll kid at the Day of Judgment.

**TYRONE**
*Impatiently.*
You know damned well it isn't kidding. You're not a fool. You can tell.

**JOSIE**
*Kiddingly.*
All right, then, I'm beautiful and you love me—in your fashion.

**TYRONE**
"In my fashion," eh? Was I reciting poetry to you? That must have been hard to take.

**JOSIE**
It wasn't. I liked it. It was all about beautiful nights and the romance of the moon.

**TYRONE**
Well, there was some excuse for that, anyway. It sure was a beautiful night. I'll never forget it.

**JOSIE**
I'm glad, Jim.

**TYRONE**
What other bunk did I pull on you—or I mean, did old John Barley-corn pull?

**JOSIE**
Not much. You were mostly quiet and sad—in a kind of daze, as if the moon was in your wits as well as whiskey.

**TYRONE**
I remember I was having a grand time at the Inn, celebrating with Phil, and then suddenly, for no reason, all the fun went out of it, and I was more melancholy than ten Hamlets.

*He pauses.*

Hope I didn't tell you the sad story of my life and weep on your bosom, Josie.

JOSIE

You didn't. The one thing you talked a lot about was that you wanted the night with me to be different from all the other nights you'd spent with women.

TYRONE

*With revulsion.*

God, don't make me think of those tramps now!

*Then with deep, grateful feeling.*

It sure was different, Josie. I may not remember much, but I know how different it was from the way I feel now. None of my usual morning-after stuff—the damned sick remorse that makes you wish you'd died in your sleep so you wouldn't have to face the rotten things you're afraid you said and did the night before, when you were so drunk you didn't know what you were doing.

JOSIE

There's nothing you said or did last night for you to regret. You can take my word for it.

TYRONE

*As if he hadn't heard—slowly.*

It's hard to describe how I feel. It's a new one on me. Sort of at peace with myself and this lousy life—as if all my sins had been forgiven—

*He becomes self-conscious—cynically.*

Nuts with that sin bunk, but you know what I mean.

JOSIE

*Tensely.*

I do, and I'm happy you feel that way, Jim.

*A pause. She goes on.*

You talked about how you'd watched too many dawns come creeping grayly over dirty windowpanes, with some tart snoring beside you—

TYRONE

*Winces.*

Have a heart. Don't remind me of that now, Josie. Don't spoil this dawn!

*A pause. She watches him tensely. He turns slowly to face the east, where the sky is now glowing with all the colors of an exceptionally beautiful sunrise. He stares, drawing a deep breath. He is profoundly moved but immediately becomes self-conscious and tries to sneer it off—cynically.*

God seems to be putting on quite a display. I like Belasco better. Rise of curtain, Act-Four stuff.

*Her face has fallen into lines of bitter hurt, but he adds quickly and angrily.*

God damn it! Why do I have to pull that lousy stuff?

*With genuine deep feeling.*

God, it's beautiful, Josie! I—I'll never forget it—here with you.

JOSIE

*Her face clearing—simply.*

I'm glad, Jim. I was hoping you'd feel beauty in it—by way of a token.

TYRONE

*Watching the sunrise—mechanically.*

Token of what?

JOSIE

Oh, I don't know. Token to me that—never mind. I forget what I meant.

*Abruptly changing the subject.*

Don't think I woke you just to admire the sunrise. You're on a farm, not Broadway, and it's time for me to start work, not go to bed.

*She gets to her feet and stretches. There is a growing strain behind her free-and-easy manner.*

And that's a hint, Jim. I can't stay entertaining you. So go back to the Inn, that's a good boy. I know you'll understand the reason, and not think I'm tired of your company.

*She forces a smile.*

TYRONE

*Gets up.*

Of course, I understand.

*He pauses—then blurts out guiltily.*

One more question. You're sure I didn't get out of order last night—and try to make you, or anything like that.

JOSIE

You didn't. You kidded back when I kidded you, the way we always do. That's all.

TYRONE

Thank God for that. I'd never forgive myself if—I wouldn't have asked you except I've pulled some pretty rotten stuff when I was drawing a blank.

*He becomes conscious of the forgotten drink he has in his hand.*

Well, I might as well drink this. The bar at the Inn won't be open for hours.

*He drinks—then looks pleasantly surprised.*

I'll be damned! That isn't Phil's rotgut. That's real, honest-to-God bonded Bourbon. Where—

*This clicks in his mind and suddenly he remembers everything and* JOSIE *sees that he does. The look of guilt and shame and anguish settles over his face. Instinctively he throws the glass away, his first reaction one of loathing for the drink which brought back memory. He feels* JOSIE *staring at him and fights desperately to control his voice and expression.*

Real Bourbon. I remember now you said a bootlegger gave it to Phil. Well, I'll run along and let you do your work. See you later, Josie.

*He turns toward the road.*

JOSIE

*Strickenly.*

No! Don't Jim! Don't go like that! You won't see me later. You'll never see me again now, and I know that's best for us both, but I can't bear to have you ashamed you wanted my love to comfort your sorrow—when I'm so proud I could give it.

*Pleadingly.*

I hoped, for your sake, you wouldn't remember, but now you do, I want you to remember my love for you gave you peace for a while.

TYRONE
*Stares at her, fighting with himself. He stammers defensively.*
I don't know what you're talking about. I don't remember—

JOSIE
*Sadly.*
All right, Jim. Neither do I then. Good-bye, and God bless you.
*She turns as if to go up the steps into the house.*

TYRONE
*Stammers.*
Wait, Josie!
*Coming to her.*
I'm a liar! I'm a louse! Forgive me, Josie. I do remember! I'm glad I remember! I'll never forget your love!
*He kisses her on the lips.*
Never!
*Kissing her again.*
Never, do you hear! I'll always love you, Josie.
*He kisses her again.*
Good-bye—and God bless you!
*He turns away and walks quickly down the road off left without looking back. She stands, watching him go, for a moment, then she puts her hands over her face, her head bent, and sobs.* HOGAN *comes out of her room and stands on top of the steps. He looks after* TYRONE *and his face is hard with bitter anger.*

JOSIE
*Sensing his presence, stops crying and lifts her head—dully.*
I'll get your breakfast in a minute, Father.

HOGAN
To hell with my breakfast! I'm not a pig that has no other thought but eating!
*Then pleadingly.*
Listen, darlin'. All you said about my lying and scheming, and what I

hoped would happen, is true. But it wasn't his money, Josie. I did see it was the last chance—the only one left to bring the two of you to stop your damned pretending, and face the truth that you loved each other. I wanted you to find happiness—by hook or crook, one way or another, what did I care how? I wanted to save him, and I hoped he'd see that only your love could— It was his talk of the beauty he saw in you that made me hope— And I knew he'd never go to bed with you even if you'd let him unless he married you. And if I gave a thought to his money at all, that was the least of it, and why shouldn't I want to have you live in ease and comfort for a change, like you deserve, instead of in this shanty on a lousy farm, slaving for me?

*He pauses—miserably.*

Can't you believe that's the truth, Josie, and not feel so bitter against me?

JOSIE

*Her eyes still following* TYRONE—*gently.*

I know it's the truth, Father. I'm not bitter now. Don't be afraid I'm going to leave you. I only said it to punish you for a while.

HOGAN

*With humble gratitude.*

Thank God for that, darlin'.

JOSIE

*Forces a teasing smile and a little of her old manner.*

A ginger-haired, crooked old goat like you to be playing Cupid!

HOGAN

*His face lights up joyfully. He is almost himself again—ruefully.*

You had me punished, that's sure. I was thinking after you'd gone I'd drown myself in Harder's ice pond. There was this consolation in it, I know that the bastard would never look at a piece of ice again without remembering me.

*She doesn't hear this. Her thoughts are on the receding figure of* TYRONE *again.* HOGAN *looks at her sad face worriedly—gently.*

Don't, darlin'. Don't be hurting yourself.

*Then as she still doesn't hear, he puts on his old, fuming irascible tone.*

Are you going to moon at the sunrise forever, and me with the sides of my stomach knocking together?

JOSIE
*Gently.*
Don't worry about me, Father. It's over now. I'm not hurt. I'm only sad for him.

HOGAN
For him?
*He bursts out in a fit of smoldering rage.*
May the blackest curse from the pit of hell—

JOSIE
*With an anguished cry.*
Don't, Father! I love him!

HOGAN
*Subsides, but his face looks sorrowful and old—dully.*
I didn't mean it. I know whatever happened he meant no harm to you. It was life I was cursing—
*With a trace of his natural manner.*
And, be God, that's a waste of breath, if it does deserve it.
*Then as she remains silent—miserably.*
Or maybe I was cursing myself for a damned old scheming fool, like I ought to.

JOSIE
*Turns to him, forcing a teasing smile.*
Look out. I might say Amen to that.
*Gently.*
Don't be sad, Father. I'm all right—and I'm well content here with you.
*Forcing her teasing manner again.*
Sure, living with you has spoilt me for any other man, anyway. There'd never be the same fun or excitement.

HOGAN
*Plays up to this—in his fuming manner.*

There'll be excitement if I don't get my breakfast soon, but it won't be fun, I'm warning you!

JOSIE

*Forcing her usual reaction to his threats.*
Och, don't be threatening me, you bad-tempered old tick. Let's go in the house and I'll get your damned breakfast.

HOGAN

Now you're talking.
*He goes in the house through her room. She follows him as far as the door—then turns for a last look down the road.*

JOSIE

*Her face sad, tender and pitying—gently.*
May you have your wish and die in your sleep soon, Jim, darling. May you rest forever in forgiveness and peace.
*She turns slowly and goes back into the house.*

CURTAIN

Eugene O'Neill (1888–1953) was born in New York City, the son of James O'Neill, a popular actor, and Mary Ellen Quinlan. During his childhood years he lived mainly in hotels with his family, following the tours of his father's company; the only permanent home the young O'Neill knew was a summer cottage in New London, Connecticut, which later became the setting for *Long Day's Journey into Night*.

As an adolescent, O'Neill attended eastern preparatory schools and then Princeton University for one year until he was expelled. During the next five years he worked as a gold prospector, a sailor, an actor, and a reporter.

O'Neill began writing plays in 1913, and by 1916 his one-act play *Bound East for Cardiff* was produced in New York by the Provincetown Players, a group he had helped found. In 1920 his full-length play *Beyond the Horizon* was produced in New York and won O'Neill the first of his four Pulitzer Prizes. During decades of extraordinary productivity, O'Neill published 24 other full-length plays. After receiving the Nobel Prize for literature in 1936, he published two of his most highly acclaimed plays, *The Iceman Cometh* and *A Moon for the Misbegotten*. O'Neill died in Boston in 1953. *Long Day's Journey into Night*, often regarded as his finest work, was published three years after his death.